INTERNATIONAL MISSION

Transformative Rethinking

INTERNATIONAL MISSIONARY COUNCIL CENTENARY SERIES

Transformative Rethinking:
Christian Mission and Cooperation in a Multireligious Indian Society

Edited by
Chongpongmeren Jamir and H. Lalrinthanga

Copyright © World Council of Churches 2024

First published 2024 by Regnum Books International
This edition is published under license from the World Council of Churches

Regnum is an imprint of the Oxford Centre for Mission Studies
St. Philip and St. James Church
Woodstock Road
Oxford, OX2 6HR, UK
www.regnumbooks.net

The rights of the World Council of Churches to be identified
as the editor of this work has been asserted by them
in accordance with the Copyright, Designs and Patents Act 1988.

All rights reserved. No part of this publication may be reproduced, stored in a retrieval system, or transmitted, in any form or by any means, electronic, mechanical, photocopying, recording or otherwise, without the prior permission of the publisher or a license permitting restricted copying. In the UK such licenses are issued by the Copyright Licensing Agency, 90 Tottenham Court Road, London W1P 9HE.

British Library Cataloguing in Publication Data
A catalogue record for this book is available from the British Library

ISBN: 979-8-8898-3885-2
eBook ISBN: 979-8-8898-3886-9

Typeset by Words by Design
www.wordsbydesign.co.uk

This series has been published with the financial support of EMW and CWME

Distributed by Fortress Press in the US, Canada, India, and Brazil

Series Preface

This series of books arises from a study process that marked the centenary of the International Missionary Council (IMC), founded in 1921 at Lake Mohonk, USA. It has its origin in the Commission on World Mission and Evangelism of the World Council of Churches, which wanted to celebrate the work of its historical predecessor IMC (1921-1961). In 2020, it therefore initiated a global and ecumenical study process, which was strongly supported by the Oxford Centre for Mission Studies (OCMS) in the UK and the Association of Protestant Churches and Missions in Germany (EMW) in Hamburg. The 18-month study process involved some 15 academic and ecumenical study centres or groups around the world, practically in all eight regions of the World Council of Churches, paying special attention to those sectors which were not represented at Lake Mohonk a hundred years earlier.

The International Missionary Council Centenary Series edited by the steering committee of the process in cooperation with the director of the CWME of the WCC presents the most interesting parts of the study process. The IMC was founded to foster mission cooperation and unity, and the study process wanted to identify important topics and challenges for mission and mission cooperation, not only in the past, even if the history of the IMC is to be celebrated, but also in the present and future. The steering committee of the study process was delighted to discover that some previously unheard voices have been heard through the process. Indeed, in order to honour the legacy of the IMC, the study process itself was implemented in an interactive and inclusive way that produced more mission cooperation and more unity among various actors in academy, church and mission bodies.

The volumes in the International Missionary Council Centenary Series present mainly, but not only, regional aspects and dimensions of world mission that has become polyphonic. The polyphonic character of mission opens and offers new common spaces for discussion and reflection on how all actors, churches, academy, mission bodies and transnational networks, can work together in creative and innovative ways, both in missiology and mission practice.

This Regnum Series builds on three foundational books that were generated by the study process and published by WCC Publications in 2022-23. A comprehensive Jubilee volume appeared as Risto Jukko ed., *Together in the Mission of God: Jubilee Reflections on the International Missionary Council*, Geneva: WCC Publications, 2022. Additionally, two mission studies anthologies gathered up the initial fruits of the study process: Risto Jukko ed., *A Hundred Years of Mission Cooperation: the Impact of the International Missionary Council 1921-2021*, Geneva: WCC Publications, 2022; and Risto Jukko ed., *The Future of Mission Cooperation: the Living Legacy of the International Missionary Council*, Geneva: WCC Publications, 2023. Now the Regnum Series offers a much more extensive harvest of the work completed by the study centres which collaborated in the IMC centenary study process.

The steering committee is delighted to be able to make the results of the study process accessible to a wider readership while recognising that opinions expressed in the book chapters are those of their authors and claim no wider authority.

Series Editors:

Marina Ngursangzeli Behera
Michael Biehl
Risto Jukko
Kenneth R. Ross
Tito Paredes
Peter Cruchley
Jingqin Gu

Contents

Introduction
  Chongpongmeren Jamir 1

I. THE INTERNATIONAL MISSIONARY COUNCIL AND INDIAN CHRISTIANITY

Historical Survey of Shifts in Mission Cooperation in India:
  Past and Present
  Arvind Kumar 9
The Indian Christian Predicament: Mapping the Reception of the
  Christian Unity and Mission Cooperation in India's Contextual
  Realities and Beyond
  Kaholi Zhimomi 23
The Enhancement the IMC Tambaram 1938 Furnished Towards India's
  Independence
  Ajay Chakraborty 35

II. UNITY, COOPERATION AND DIALOGUE

Proposal for "Informal Dialogue": Christian Witness in the Context
  of Hindu-Majority India
  John Arun Kumar 49
Church and Social Justice: Consensus with the Holy Spirit
  E.D. Solomon 61
Cooperation and Unity among the Mission Churches in Mizoram
  H. Lalrinthanga 75
Ecumenical Continuity of Missions: The Working Principles and
  Objectives of the International Missionary Council and the
  Lairam Isua Krista Baptist Kohhran
  Zadingluaia Chinzah 85
Relationship of Churches in the Mission Fields in Northeast India:
  Prospects and Challenges
  Lalfakawma Ralte 97

III. MISSION THEOLOGY AND THEOLOGICAL FORMATION

From Ad Gentes to New Evangelization:
  Roman Catholic Missionary Trajectories
  Francis Thonippara 107
Decolonial Reading of the Context of Mission in Northeast India
  Taimaya Ragui 117
Whither Theological Formation in India?
  Chongpongmeren Jamir 133

Notes on Contributors 147

Introduction

Chongpongmeren Jamir

No personal relationship will be true and permanent that is not built on a spiritual basis. India is a land that has a "religious atmosphere."[1]

V.S. Azariah made this statement in one of the evening sessions of the World Missionary Conference at Edinburgh in 1910. In such a land, he continues, "the easiest point of contact with the heart is on the spiritual side."[2] Though more than a century has passed since Azariah spoke, religion continues to pull at the heartstrings of Indian society. How to witness to Christ in a multireligious society continues to be the overarching concern for Indian churches and missions today.

The chapters in this volume are papers presented during the regional consultations of the IMC/CWME Centenary Study Process, 2021-2022, in India. The overall goal of the study process was to identify key themes and tasks of mission and for cooperation in mission in the present and the future. The participants at the regional consultations observed that nationalism and related issues such as indigenization, self-determination and nation-building play a leading role in mission and ecumenical discussions in India. They also observed that the current trend of politics and faith in India is dominated by the majority-minority discourse advocated by the radical Hindu political organizations, which leaves the churches in India grappling with issues of religious freedom, communal harmony, poverty, social and political exploitation in the context of the plurality of faiths practiced by the people in the region.[3] Thus, the question of how to engage in Christian mission and cooperation in a multi-religious society provided the framework for investigation. A key element in the study process was the analysis of the attitude of the "others" (that is, non-Christians) towards Christian mission and ecumenism in India, which was not seen as complimentary. Thus, participants expressed the need for a critical rethinking of the way we think of Christian mission and its practices and theology. Indian Christianity has a rich tradition of engaging in rethinking mission and theology (no less represented in the seminal work *Rethinking Christianity in India*[4]). While drawing inspiration from this heritage, the participants also realized that

---

[1] V.S. Azariah, "The Problem of Cooperation between Foreign and Native Workers," in *World Missionary Conference, 1910: The History and Records of the Conference* (Edinburgh/London: Oliphant, Anderson and Ferrier, 1910), 314.
[2] *Ibid.*
[3] Report of the ATC-UTC-SAIACS-Conference in the IMC Centenary Study Process 2021-22.
[4] G.V. Job, P. Chenchiah, V. Chakkarai, et al., *Rethinking Christianity in India*. (Madras: A.N. Sudarisanam, 1939).

the critical need of the hour is to look within ourselves for a transformative experience.

The contributions in this volume are based on the particular interests of individual scholars and their theological assumptions and locations within an ecclesiastical tradition, each allowed to express themselves without attempting to monitor them. The contributors were bound together in this collective endeavour by a conscious reflection on the impact of the IMC process, directly or indirectly, on Christianity in India. Accordingly, the chapters in the volume are arranged under three descriptors: i) The International Missionary Council and Indian Christianity; ii) Unity, Cooperation and Dialogue; and iii) Mission Theology and Theological Formation. Each descriptor highlights the impact of the IMC process in the history, practice and thought of Christianity in India.

The nineteenth century saw the development of two streams of thought in India contributing to Christian mission thinking in the region. The first was concerned with the need for cooperation in Christian missions. In this regard, several regional and national conferences were held in India over the nineteenth century to promote Christian fellowship and cooperation in mission, the first of which was held in Bombay (present-day Mumbai) in 1825.[5] The second stream was concerned with the need for an Indian church devoid of its Western bearings, including denominationalism. The formation of the Hindu Church of the Lord Jesus Christ in 1858, the Bengal Christian Association in 1868 and the National Church of Madras in 1886 were expressions of the aspiration of Indian churches for autonomy.[6] The two streams came together in the church union movement in India, starting with the merger of Presbyterian and Congregationalist churches in South India in 1908. Thus, in India, mission cooperation and church indigenization programmes are intertwined with each other. In Chapter 1, Arvind Kumar discusses how mission cooperation in India emerged in the context of the nineteenth-century Christian mission in India and how it got further impetus from the IMC process. Since the nineteenth century, cooperation among churches, mission agencies and institutions in India has provided a sense of unity geared towards a common cause of evangelism, justice and peace. However, Kumar posits that the communal spirit that helped overcome denominational differences also brought challenges that undermined Christian unity. Thus, he calls for a "praxis-oriented cooperation" to deal with the vices that hinder the spirit of unity in the Indian churches.

Edinburgh 1910 and the subsequent development of the IMC in 1921 was a process where various streams of existing voices of mission cooperation and unity in various parts of the world came together into a global movement. In Chapter 2, Kaholi Zhimomi discusses the reception of Christian mission and ecumenism in the church and society in India. Within the specific context of early twentieth-century India, which was experiencing a rise in nationalism, anything associated with the western colonizers or their land was looked upon

---

[5] Eber Priestly, *The Church of South India: Adventure in Union* (London: Church of South India Council in Great Britain, 1970), 7.
[6] Leonard Fernando and G. Gispert-Sauch, *Christianity in India: Two Thousand Years of Faith* (New Delhi: Viking/Penguin Books, 2004), 247.

Introduction 3

with suspicion. Thus, even the urgent call for Christian unity in the ecumenical movement was met with misunderstandings by both Christians and non-Christians.[7] Zhimomi argues that though the ecumenical movement has achieved significant success in India, its true vision is yet to be fully realized. Thus, she proposes a transformative ecumenism to help overcome the inherent binaries of "self and other" and redefines the theology of ecumenism from the perspective of the excluded and the otherized.

In the build-up to India's independence in 1947, the identification of the Christian faith as the religion of the colonizers, coupled with the lethargic response of many Christians to the call of the national movement, put Indian Christians in a predicament in the identity mapping in India. As the national movement intensified, Christians in India were caught in a dilemma[8] – should they be involved in the political movement? If so, to what extent should they be involved? In religious terms, they asked, what is Christianity to/for India? On one level, it led to a rethinking of Christianity in the Indian culture. On another, it led to a call for self-determination and autonomy in the Indian churches. In Chapter 3, Ajay Chakraborty discusses how the discussions in the IMCs, particularly at Tambaram in 1938, shaped the Indian Christian attitude towards the Indian national movement. He argues that Tambaram 1938 transformed the mission-oriented leaders in India into nationalist or pro-independence leaders.

The twentieth-century context of rising nationalism in India provided a dialogical locus to mission and theological thinking in India.[9] Relations with people of other faiths emerged as a key concern. Already in the IMCs at Jerusalem in 1928 and Tambaram in 1938, India provided the background for discussions on interreligious dialogue. Indian contributions to conversations on interreligious dialogue continued in the post-independence period through the works of Indian ecumenical theologians. The participants of the regional consultation observed that the focus of earlier mission and theological thinking on interreligious dialogue had been on a formal format. However, in the current political climate, such efforts suffer from a lack of reciprocity from the dominant Hindu community.[10] In Chapter 4, John Arun Kumar argues that in the current political climate in India, while formal interreligious dialogue is commendable, an informal approach would be more feasible. This is not a mere reactionary response, as Kumar argues, as the interaction between people of different religions is a daily reality in India and that Indians of all faiths desire to live harmoniously with each other. In Chapter 5, E.D. Solomon presents a real-life example of interreligious engagement in India. He argues that the concept of

---

[7] Kaj Baago, *Pioneers of Indigenous Christianity* (Mysore: Weseley, 1969), 1-2.
[8] Kaj Baago, *A History of the National Christian Council of India* (Madras: CLS, 1965), 28.
[9] Chongpongmeren Jamir, "Christian Mission and Cooperation in a Multireligious Context: Mapping the Impact of the IMC/CWME Movement in Rethinking Mission Theology and Practice in India," in *A Hundred Years of Mission Cooperation: The Impact of the International Missionary Council 1921-2021*, ed. Risto Jukko (Geneva: WCC Publications, 2022), 168.
[10] Report of the ATC-UTC-SAIACS-Conference in the IMC Centenary Study Process 2021-22.

Edinburgh 1910 is a historical landmark in Christian mission and mission theology. Here starts a dynamic process that invites churches and mission agencies to reflect on the changing context and reinvent mission practice and theology. Though the event at Edinburgh 1910 was a Protestant affair, the mission discussions that came out of it were represented by wider Christian traditions. For the Roman Catholic Church, the Second Vatican Council (1962-65) was a turning point, a landmark in defining the contemporary Catholic mission and relations with others, both Christians and non-Christians.[13] In Chapter 9, Francis Thonippara traces the Catholic missionary trajectory in India with reference to papal encyclicals on evangelization since the Second Vatican Council. He argues that timely papal interventions, the teaching of New Evangelization in particular, have given vitality and new directions to the mission commitments of the Roman Catholic Church worldwide, including India.

At Edinburgh 1910 and the subsequent missionary conferences, the "younger churches" received intense attention, providing a conducive environment for the emergence of contextual theologies in Asia and Africa.[14] The IMC's initiation of the Theological Education Fund (TEF) in 1958 further provided an impetus to the development of contextual theology in various parts of the world, including Dalit and Tribal theologies in India. A key concern of the proponents of these theologies has been on the decolonization of Christian theology in India, which they lamented was a "xerox-copy", "duplicate", "carbon-copy" or "replica" of Western Theology.[15] In Chapter 10, Taimaya Ragui posits that the adoration of all things colonial continues to influence Christian theology in northeast India. Therefore, he argues for a rethinking of Christian theology in the region taking into consideration the "multiple contexts" of the tribal-indigenous people.

Great stress was laid at Edinburgh 1910 on the importance of the theological formation of missionaries for their task.[16] The IMC and its regional constituent, the National Christian Council of India, Burma and Ceylon, were pioneers in the advocacy of providing quality theological education in India. The two

---

[13] Adam Deville, "Church," in *The Oxford Handbook of Ecumenical Studies*, eds. Geoffrey Wainwright and Paul McPartlan (Oxford: Oxford University Press, 2021), 225. Also see Cassidy, Edward Idris Cardinal. *Rediscovering Vatican II: Ecumenism and Interreligious Dialogue*. (NY: Paulist Press, 2005).
[14] Dietrich Werner, "Theological Education in the Changing Context of World Christianity – an Unfinished Agenda," *International Bulletin of Missionary Research* 35:2 (April 2011), 96; H.S. Wilson, "Theological Education and Ecumenical Challenges in Asia," in *Asian Handbook for Theological Education and Ecumenism*, ed. Hope Antone et al (Oxford: Regnum, 2013), 628.
[15] Renthy Keitzar, "Theology Today" in *In Search of Praxis Theology for the Nagas*, ed. V.K. Nuh (New Delhi: Regency, 2003), 21. *Cf.* David Joy and Joseph Duggan eds. *Decolonizing the Body of Christ: Theology and Theory after Empire?* (NY: Palgrave Macmillan, 2012); Wati A. Longchar, *An Emerging Asian Theology: Tribal Theology Issues, Method and Perspective*. (Jorhat: TSC, 2000); Rocky, R.L. "Tribes and Tribal Studies in North East: Deconstructing the Politics of Colonial Methodology" in *Journal of Tribal Intellectual Collective India* 1:2 (2013) 25-37.
[16] Werner, "Theological Education in the Changing Context of World Christianity – an Unfinished Agenda," 92.

collaborated in initiating the Commission on Christian Higher Education in India and Burma in 1930, which was tasked with assessing Christian education in India, including theological education. Later from 1940-1945, the National Christian Council conducted "The Survey of Theological Education in India" aimed at producing a standard plan for theological education in India. Thus, the IMC process has played a key role in promoting quality theological formation in India. Given the tradition of the IMC in India, the present study process would be incomplete without drawing our attention to the theological formation and what we might learn from the study to help shape the future curricula of theological education in India. In Chapter 11, Chongpongmeren Jamir reflects on the future of theological education in India in the light of the findings of the regional consultations. He argues the need for theological educators and institutions to work together towards setting common standards for theological education in India and to play the prophetic role of preparing/equipping the whole people of God to engage effectively with contemporary realities in society.

The understanding and expression of Christian mission have evolved in different ways in India and elsewhere since the formation of the IMC in 1921. Churches in India have, from time to time, engaged in rethinking what mission theology and practice would be biblically and contextually relevant in the region. The changing political-cultural dynamics in India once again call for a fresh reflection on Christian mission and cooperation, relations with other faiths and engagement with society. The study process was an opportune time for those involved, to engage in a *metanoia*, a transformative reflection on how we think of ourselves as Indian Christians and on how we do mission. The insights shared, questions raised and proposals made in this volume are humble attempts towards engaging in a transformative rethinking of Christian mission and cooperation in India.

consensus in the *gram panchayat* system in India can provide a framework to develop a theology of mission for the church's involvement in conflict resolution involving other religious communities. Reflecting on a funeral at Ahamrai village, he discerns the role of the Holy Spirit in facilitating consensus and a spirit of solidarity with the bereaved.

Marina Ngursangzeli Behera has shown that in Northeast India, unlike in the other parts of India, "at the time of the founding years of the IMC, there were interconnected developments but not direct interaction" with the IMC process.[11] In Chapter 6, H. Lalrinthanga shows how the spirit of the IMC process was played out in the mission churches in Mizoram, though one cannot speak of direct interaction with the global movement. The Presbyterian, Baptist and Evangelical (Lakher) churches in the region showed remarkable commitment to cooperation and unity in the life and mission of the churches through collaborative action in Bible translation, publication of hymn books and exchange of delegates in presbytery meetings. In Chapter 7, Zadingluaia Chinzah asks, "What is the relation between the event at Lawngtlai, Mizoram, 1999, and the event at Lake Mohonk, New York, 1921?" Despite the time-space that separates the two events, he argues that the church union movement that led to the formation of the Lairam Isua Krista Baptist Kohhran (LIKBK) at Lawngtlai resonates with ecumenical concerns raised in the IMC meeting at Lake Mohonk, and later at Jerusalem, Madras, Whitby and Willingen. The two studies from Northeast India show how the discussions on Christian mission and cooperation in the IMC process have found praxis in various parts of the world.

The question of what a global movement like the IMC, separated by time and space, has to do with local churches and missions is not only a historical question but also a missiological one. In Chapter 8, Lalfakawma Ralte explores the continuing relevance of the IMC discussions for Christian mission today. The cordiality and cooperation exhibited by Christian missionaries of various traditions in Mizoram is a remarkable story of what is possible in an ecumenical relationship (see Chapter 6). However, Ralte's study shows that Mizo Presbyterian (The Presbyterian Church of India, Mizoram Synod, PCIMS) and Baptist (Baptist Church of Mizoram, BCM) missionaries working in the neighbouring state of Arunachal Pradesh today have taken a different trajectory. He argues that the cooperation between the two mission agencies is hampered by a lack of direction and harmonization among its diverse actors and participants. Thus, he asked, what might PCIMS and BCM missions and mission churches in Arunachal Pradesh learn from past missionary cooperation towards developing a stronger awareness of ecumenism among mission agencies and in missionary formation?[12] Therefore, ecumenical formation in training for missionary service is necessary to foster cooperation in Christian missions.

---

[11] Marina Ngursangzeli Behera, "Mission in Northeast India in the Early 20th Century: A Perspective from the Global South on the Founding of the IMC in the Global North," in *A Hundred Years of Mission Cooperation: The Impact of the International Missionary Council 1921-2021*, ed. Risto Jukko (Geneva: WCC Publications, 2022), 86.

[12] Anne-Marie Kool, "Changing Images in the Formation for Mission: Commission Five in Light of Current Challenges, A World Perspective" in *Edinburgh 2010: Mission Then and Now*, eds. David A. Kerr and Kenneth R. Ross (Oxford: Regnum, 2009), 164.

I. The International Missionary Council and Indian Christianity

2. THE INTERNATIONAL MISSIONARY COUNCIL
AND INDIAN CHRISTIANITY

Historical Survey of Shifts in Mission Cooperation in India: Past and Present

Arvind Kumar

As the modern missionary movement expanded in the nineteenth century, a sense of competition arose among the various missionary societies. The subsequent disunity led to innumerable failures and contextual challenges in the mission field. In such a context, missionaries felt the need for mutual sharing and discussion of problems and difficulties they faced in the mission field.[1] They realized that the perpetuation of Western denominational Christianity in the mission field weakened the church's witness and hampered its effectiveness. It became clear that without cooperation between the missionaries, irrespective of their denominations, it would be difficult to face the challenges in the field.[2] Thus, they developed an urge to unite into one Christian community unhampered by denominationalism. Subsequently, several attempts were made since the nineteenth century towards fostering cooperation in Christian mission.[3] In 1805, William Carey proposed a World Missionary Conference to be held in 1810. Though it did not materialise until a century later, the desire for unity in mission was sustained through several regional conferences where missionaries from different societies in Bombay (Mumbai), Calcutta (Kolkata) and Madras (Chennai) fellowshipped together in prayer and informal discussions to resolve differences.[4] Gradually, this sense of sharing and discussion of mission-related issues gave birth to the mission cooperation movement in India. The cooperation among the various missions was instrumental in pulling down many doctrinal barriers and facilitated the effort towards Christian unity. Mission cooperation structured itself in the union of various churches and institutions all over India and continues to impact Christian mission towards effective holistic service. This contribution intends to highlight the history of the shift in mission cooperation and the pattern of mission cooperation in India.

Socio-historical Context of Mission Cooperation in India

Before the mission cooperation movement, there were serious clashes between the various Christian missions over their territorial boundaries in India. This negatively impacted the mission field, resulting in the gradual decline of mission

---

[1] T.V. Philip, "Protestant Christianity in India Since 1858," in *Christianity in India: A History in Ecumenical Perspective*, eds. H. C. Perumalil and E.R. Hambye (Alleppey: Prakasam Publications, n.d.), 293.
[2] Rajaiah D. Paul, *Ecumenism in Action: A Historical Survey of the Church of South India* (Madras: CLS, 1972), 3.
[3] *Ibid.* 4.
[4] O.L. Snaitang, "A Historical Survey of Ecumenism in India," in *Ecumenism in India Today*, ed. James Massey (Bangalore: BTESSC/ SATHRI, 2008), 12.

work. As O.L. Snaitang points out, denominational divides were contradictory to the Christian faith and a mockery to the non-Christian world when mission operations got involved in denominational mud-slinging, dividedness and "Sheep-stealing".[5] It resulted in a divided Christianity with native Christians identifying themselves as Methodists, Baptists, Presbyterians, Lutherans, Congregationalists and later Pentecostals of various streams.[6] In such a context, many felt the need for unity and cooperation between the various Christian denominations in India. In 1902, various Christian missions agreed upon a principle of "comity", which recognised certain territories for a mission society and where other societies were to abstain from entering and working.[7] This principle imputed an initial solution to the conflict among Christian denominations by delineating tentative territorial boundaries for each mission agency.

International Missionary Council and its Ecumenism

The International Missionary Council (IMC) was initiated by the continuous effort of the Continuation and the Emergency Committee of the World Missionary Conference at Edinburgh in 1910. In 1920, at the interim conference at Crans, the members agreed that national Christian councils should form an international missionary committee. The result was the formation of the IMC in 1921. It was formed to bring together national Christian Councils to a common sense of unity for a united effort in world evangelization. Administratively, it was a federation of national Christian councils.[8]

The third conference of the IMC was held at Tambaram, Chennai, in 1938 and had four hundred seventy-one delegates from sixty-nine countries. The main theme of the conference was "World Mission of the Churches." The IMC Tambaram is very significant in two ways: first, it was "a unifying event in the life of the church." It was an event that reminded the churches of the fellowship of the Church Universal. It emphasised what it was rather than what it did. Consequently, it became a model of unity and fellowship for churches of countries that had never been together till then on a continent-wide basis, such as Africa and Asia.[9] Second, it emphasized an "indestructible unity for a broken world." The Tambaram conference inadvertently prepared the world's Protestant churches for six years of devastating war and its aftermath. As one looks back after decades, this seems to have been its most significant contribution. The Tambaram conference was later declared "the Miracle of Madras" as, amid crumbling international relations, it was a miracle that the conference was held at all. In those terrifying and uncertain days leading up to the Second World War,

---

[5] O.L. Snaitang, *A History of Ecumenical Movement: An Introduction* (Bangalore: BTESSC, 2012), 66.
[6] *Ibid.* 67.
[7] C.B. Firth, *An Introduction to Indian Church History* (Delhi: ISPCK, 2005), 233.
[8] Snaitang, *A History of Ecumenical Movement*, 107-108.
[9] William Richey Hogg, *Ecumenical Foundations: A History of the International Missionary Council and its Nineteenth-Century Background* (New York: Harper Brothers, 1952), 301.

the IMC drew together men and women from various nations. For the first time in history, large groups of nationals from the soon-to-be-warring countries came together to unitedly face a common task. Such a fore-glimpse of unity strengthened Christians throughout the war worldwide.[10] Cut off from each other, often suffering persecution and hardship, the unity born at Madras was held in the most desolated years. It became a signpost of the communion and fellowship of all Christian churches worldwide.[11] Thus, the IMC Tambaram provided an opportunity for men and women from churches in remote parts of the world to be identified as world Christians sharing in universal fellowship. It was a uniting stab towards cooperation in missions in India and the world.[12]

The IMC Tambaram focused more deeply on the church (rather than missions). Its emphasis was centred upon strengthening the younger churches as part of the ongoing, universal fellowship.[13] Never before had so stirring an appeal been rung by the younger churches for cooperation.[14] It sought primarily to strengthen the upbuilding of the world Christian community by directing attention to the practical problems and programs of the churches and to provide specific recommendations for actions.[15] William Richey Hogg commented, "Madras made the church its central concern and a new sense of its reality runs through every statement produced there. As never before had been possible, members of the churches saw the Church Universal partially disclosed in their midst. In a day when many regarded the historic church as an unnecessary appendage to the 'Christian spirit,' Madras brought a new awareness of the church's importance."[16] Tambaram, in time, became a forum of cooperation at national and international levels uniting missions and churches in desolate events and times.

National Council of Churches in India and Mission Cooperation

The history of the origin of the National Council of Churches in India (NCCI) goes back to the gathering of missionaries from different denominations in India in regional and national conferences since 1855 to discuss their common problems. These conferences were the foundation on which the National Missionary Council and its local branches were built. In India, the fourth All India Missionary Conference held at Madras (Chennai) in 1902 became the first official ecumenical meeting, which appointed a board of arbitration for the whole of India. The National Missionary Society was formed in 1905, drawing together Indian Christians from different denominations. In 1913, eight provincial

---

[10] *Ibid.* 302.
[11] *Ibid.*
[12] *Ibid.* 301-302.
[13] *Ibid.* 293.
[14] *Ibid.* 301-302.
[15] *Ibid.* 294.
[16] *Ibid.* 298-299.

councils were formed in Bengal, Bihar-Orissa, Bombay, Punjab, middle India, Upper Provinces, Madras and Burma.[17]

While visiting various countries looking to set up national missionary councils, John R. Mott held meetings in India with missionaries and native Christian leaders, which led to the formation of a permanent council, the National Missionary Council of India, in 1914.[18] It was then affiliated with the IMC. In 1923 its name was changed to the National Christian Council of India, Burma and Ceylon. Later, due to political and administrative reasons, the councils of Burma and Ceylon were formed as separate independent councils.[19] In Pune, in January 1922, a new constitution for a National Christian Council was drafted, incorporating several sections directly from that of the IMC and inviting equal Indian membership in the council.[20] Then, because of an inevitable shift from mission to church in the light of India's independence, the council reorganized itself into the National Council of Churches in India (NCCI) in 1979.[21] Over the years the NCCI has become a key agency of interdenominational cooperation in India.

The stated objectives of the NCCI are "to stimulate thinking and investigation on mission questions; to enlist in the solution of these questions the best knowledge and experience, and to make results available to all Churches and Missions in India; to help to coordinate the activities of the Regional Christian Council and bring it to bear on the moral and social problems of the day."[22] In 2014, the NCCI celebrated a hundred years of ecumenism in India. Presently, the NCCI has thirty member Churches, eighteen Regional Christian Councils, eighteen All India Christian Organisations, seven related agencies and two autonomous bodies.[23] It is an inter-confessional autonomous body committed to the gospel value of justice and peace. It is a platform for promoting and coordinating various forms of ministries of witness and service in Indian society.

Historical Survey of Mission Cooperation in India

The eighteenth-century Tranquebar Mission (TM) was the first Protestant mission in India and became the stepping stone of Protestant Christianity in India. It was an interdenominational cooperation involving Danish Lutherans, German Pietists and English Anglicans.

The TM began with the King of Denmark Frederick IV, a Lutheran, employing two German Pietist missionaries, Bartholomew Ziegenbalg and

---

[17] Isaac Devadoss, "A Historical Survey of Ecumenism in India," in *Ecumenism in India Today,* ed. James Massey (Bangalore: BTESSC/SATHARI, 2008), 18.
[18] The IMC was formed in 1921 at Lake Mohonk, New York as a permanent advisory and consultative body for Protestant missions. Firth, *An Introduction to Indian Church History*, 235.
[19] *Ibid.*
[20] Hogg, *Ecumenical Foundations*, 213.
[21] Devadoss, "A Historical Survey of Ecumenism in India," 18.
[22] Firth, *An Introduction to Indian Church History*, 235.
[23] National Council of Churches in India, accessed September 15, 2021, https://ncci1914.com/introduction/.

Henry Pluetschau, from the Halle University, Germany, for mission work in India.[24] It was a cross-cultural missionary cooperation initiated for evangelical activities in India.[25] The Anglican involvement in the TM mission came through the Society for the Propagation of Christian Knowledge (SPCK), which was formed in 1698. In 1712, the SPCK extended help to the TM by sending the New Testament in Portuguese, setting up the first printing press and providing aid for maintaining and running two Lutheran elementary schools at Tranquebar. Further, the SPCK showed its commitment to the spirit of cooperation by supporting the Lutheran missionaries when Danish support was not available for the missionaries outside the Danish settlement. The Lutheran mission at Madras (Chennai) was even popularly referred to as the "English mission" in Denmark and Germany, a reflection of the key role played by the English SPCK in the TM mission.[26] Differences existed between the missions in terms of nationalities, ecclesiastical structures and doctrinal teachings. Yet, they had the spirit of mutual love, respect and trust, and worked together despite their differences.[27] The TM was, therefore, a mission of remarkable international and interdenominational cooperation with Lutheran missionaries, mostly Germans and a few Scandinavians.[28]

Indian Christians and Mission Cooperation

An in-depth study of Indian Christianity shows that Christian unity in its real sense originated on Indian soil, not from the Western missionaries. It was the protest of Indian Christians against Western denominations and missionary paternalism that led to church unity discussions in several missionary conferences in India. Several experiments in church union were also made in India by Indian Christians, such as the Christo Samaj in Calcutta, the National Christian Alliance in Western India and the National Church in Madras.[29] Furthermore, Indian Christians held several regional conferences where resolutions on working towards larger unity, if not towards one united church, were passed. The earliest such initiative was the Bengal Association for the Promotion of Christian Truth and Godliness and the Protection of the Right of Indian Christians, formed in Calcutta in 1868. Another example is the Western India Native Christian Alliance in Bombay in 1871.[30]

---

[24] M.E. Gibbs, "Anglican and Protestant Mission, 1706-1857," in *Christianity in India: A History in Ecumenical Perspective*, eds. H. C. Perumalil and E.R. Hambye (Alleppey: Prakasam Publications, n.d.), 212-213; Snaitang, *A History of Ecumenical Movement*, 64.
[25] King Fredrick IV was from Denmark and the missionaries employed were from Germany. This mission in India was financially supported by Denmark and manually executed by missionaries from Germany. This is why it can be considered a cross-cultural cooperation in mission.
[26] Snaitang, *A History of Ecumenical Movement*, 65.
[27] *Ibid.* 11-12.
[28] Gibbs, "Anglican and Protestant Mission," 213.
[29] Devadoss, "A Historical Survey of Ecumenism in India," 16.
[30] *Ibid* 17.

Though mission societies working in India had a common objective of presenting the Gospel, ecclesiastical differences and conflicting interests meant that they appeared more in contention rather than love. By the mid-nineteenth century, missionaries had realized these mistakes, and in due course, attempted to iron out Western ecclesiastical differences through mission cooperation. Various meetings and conferences resulted in the sharing of knowledge, courses and advice. It reduced misunderstandings, conflicts in mission operations and encroachment.[31]

Mission Cooperation through Conferences

In India, mission cooperation began from the local mission conferences and stimulated to the regional and national levels.

The earliest moves towards cooperation were the local mission associations in Bombay, Calcutta and Madras (c. 1825-1830). A key factor that led to the local-level cooperation was the feedback from intellectuals of other religious faiths about disunity among Christians. In 1825, the Bombay Missionary Association called for a meeting where representatives from the Church Missionary Society and the American Board of Commissioners for Foreign Missions attended. Later, they extended the invitation to all the Protestant mission societies. Similar meetings were started at Calcutta (Kolkata) and Madras (Chennai) in 1830. The main objective was to encourage ecclesiastical openness and promote interdenominational fellowship through dialogue.[32] These efforts can be considered as the early impulse at mission cooperation through mutual counsel in India.

By the mid-nineteenth century, regional ecumenical conferences were held in Northern and Southern India. In North India, conferences were held in Calcutta in 1855, Benares in 1857, and Lahore in 1863. The Baptist Missionary Society, the Church Missionary Society, the Cathedral Mission, the Church of Scotland Mission, the Free Church of Scotland, the American and Scottish Presbyterian Missions, the Methodists and the German Mission took an active part in these conferences. Missionaries from each society learned the value of unity in India and expressed their mutual love and concern in solidarity.[33] In South India, conferences were held in Ootacamund in 1858, Bangalore in 1879 and Madras in 1900. In these conferences, various issues such as "communication of the Gospel in vernacular language, education, bible translation, developing vibrant indigenous church, and issues such as caste, comity and Christian unity" were prominent.[34] Of these conferences, only the Madras meeting insisted on official representations and demanded experienced delegates for discussion and effective deliberation from the societies. These conferences boosted a sense of cooperation at a higher level and its value in relation to the vast majority of the non-Christian population.

---

[31] Snaitang, *A History of Ecumenical Movement*, p. 74.
[32] *Ibid.*
[33] Snaitang, *A History of Ecumenical Movement*, 75.
[34] *Ibid.* 76.

Mission cooperation was not limited to the local and regional levels but extended to the national level as well. The agenda for national-level cooperation was expressed in a regional conference held at Lahore in 1862. The all-India National Missionary Conferences were conducted in Allahabad from December 27, 1872 to January 1, 1873; Calcutta from December 28, 1882 to January 2, 1883; Bombay from December 29, 1892 to January 4, 1893 and Madras from December 11-18, 1902. Cooperation grew rapidly among the missionaries, with an increasing number of societies participating in the conferences year by year.[35] The gatherings formed an arena where people shared ideas and offered proposals for advancing Christian work.[36]

These meetings revealed a growing spirit of cooperation among the various Christian missions in a variety of ways. Church union was not an aim at these conferences, but everyone was conscious of their lack of oneness and the common challenge they faced. V. S. Azariah saw denominational church disunity as a hindrance to evangelization: "Disunion in the mission field ... is an offense and stumbling block to the non-Christian; a perplexity and a problem to the Christian; and a cause of wastage and inefficiency to the missionary cause." He further commented that "cooperation between the foreign and native church workers can only result from a proper relationship ... In India, the relationship too often is not what it ought to be, and things must change, and change speedily if there is to be a large measure of hearty cooperation between the foreign missionaries and the Indian workers."[37] Mission conferences became the fountain of setting right the relationship between the native Christians and missionaries and enriching the taste of mission cooperation in Indian mission enterprises.

Institutional Cooperation

Another very important cooperation that took place in India was the "Union Institution". It began in the nineteenth century but became more common in the twentieth century. This cooperation involved the running of secular and theological colleges and other institutions by two or more missions in partnership. The extension of cooperation within the field of education, medical work and theological education became a unique feature of the ecumenical movement.

---

[35] Church Missionary Intelligencers: A Monthly Journal of Missionary Information 18 (London: Church Missionary Society, 1893), 173.
[36] Snaitang, *A History of Ecumenical Movement*, 74-78; Richard V. Pierard, "The Ecumenical Movement and The Missionary Movement: You Can't Have One Without the Other", accessed September 1, 2021, http://edinburgh2010.org/fileadmin/files/edinburgh2010/files/Resources/UBS%20Pierard%20-%20The%20Ecumenical%20Movement %20and%20Missionary%20Movement.pdf.
[37] V.S. Azariah, "The Problem of Cooperation between Foreign and Native Worker," in *Ecumenical Movement: An Anthology of Key Texts and Voices*, ed. Michael Kinnamon (Geneva: World Council of Churches, 2016), 267.

Cooperation in the Educational Field

An early example of Christian mission cooperation in the field of education was the Madras Christian College, reorganized in 1887 as a joint enterprise with the entry of the Church Mission Society and the Wesleyan Methodist Missionary Society into a partnership with the Free Church of Scotland Mission, which had looked after it on its own until then. Another example was the Wesleyan Methodist Missionary Society's collaboration with sister societies in a Christian college for Women in Madras (Chennai).[38] The partnership of these above-stated societies strengthened the institutions financially, enabled the appointment of highly trained teachers, and provided ample provisions for buildings and equipment. Where it might have been difficult or even impossible for each mission to staff, equip and maintain an institution on its own, several missions together were able to maintain one jointly.[39]

Cooperation in the Medical Field

Institutional cooperation was not limited to only educational institutions but extended to professional colleges and institutions, especially in the medical field. The All-India Mission Tuberculosis Sanatorium, Arogyavaram, the Christian Medical College, Vellore, the Christian Medical College, Ludhiana and the Emmanuel Hospital Association would never have been possible without the cooperation among various Christian missions in India.[40] The cooperation in the healthcare division strengthened the humanitarian service in India.

Cooperation in the Theological Field

Cooperation in the theological institutions was another unique shift in mission cooperation in India. At the beginning of the nineteenth century, theological colleges such as Serampore College, Serampore, founded in 1818 by the Baptists and Union Theological Seminary, Bareilly, founded in 1860 by the Methodist Episcopal Church, were already existing. However, the first theological college that came into being through the cooperation of various missions was the United Theological College (UTC), Bangalore, founded in 1910. The words of W.H. Campbell recorded a sense of a shift in the thinking of missionaries:

> There is a great need for more cultured and forceful men in the native ministry, who may successfully address their fellow countrymen; for Indian Christian scholars, who, nurtured on the various leaning of the East and West, shall interpret the practical West to the philosophic East and be held to show the religion of Christ is in accord with the best sentiments of India's best minds.[41]

The UTC began with the cooperation of different societies called together by J. Duthie of Nagercoil in June 1906. The different mission societies incorporated

---

[38] Vijay Kumar, "Ecumenical Cooperation of the Missions in Karnataka (India), 1834-1989: A Historical Analysis of the Evangelistic Strategy of the Missions" (PhD diss., Lutheran School of Theology, Chicago, 1996), 109-110.
[39] Firth, *An Introduction to Indian Church History*, 237.
[40] *Ibid.*
[41] W.H. Campbell, Quoted in the "United Theological College of South India and Ceylon, March 1911" (UTC Archives, File No. 1), 1.

to form UTC were the United Free Church of Scotland, the American Arcot Mission, the American Board of Commissioners for Foreign Missions, the Wesleyan Methodist Society and the London Missionary Society.[42] The Tamilnadu Theological Seminary was the first fruit of the talks on ecumenical relations between the Church of South India (CSI) and the Lutheran Churches in Tamil Nadu in 1969. The establishment of the Federated Faculty for Research and Culture (FFRRC) in Kerala in 1980 is a form of institutional unity among the theological fraternity of the Orthodox, Mar Thoma and CSI theological institutions in Kerala.[43]

Church Union: An Organic Cooperation

Mission cooperation led to the Church Union movement in India in the first decade of the twentieth century, resulting in the formation of the Church of South India (CSI) in 1947, the Church of North India (CNI) in 1970 and the North East India Christian Council (NEICC) in 1962. This mega-cooperation changed the whole scenario of the life and ministry of the Indian churches towards indigeneity.

Conciliar Cooperation:
Collaboration of CSI, CNI and the Mar Thoma Church

A new attempt towards a wider union was initiated with the inauguration of the CNI. The CNI sent out invitations to churches to start negotiations for greater cooperation. The CSI and the Mar Thoma Church accepted the invitation in 1974, and the three church bodies formed a Joint Theological Commission (JTC) with the objective of exploring the possibility of close cooperation between them. In 1976, the JTC was renamed as the Joint Council (JC). It focuses on organic oneness while retaining the autonomy and identity of the three churches. After working for several years, at the meeting in Calcutta (Kolkata) on November 11-14, 2000, the JC was renamed "The Communion of Churches in India" (CCI).

Contemporary Efforts in Mission Cooperation in India

In India, the mission cooperation movement began as a movement uniting different missions, denominations and institutions for a common task of evangelization and continues to impact contemporary Indian churches. A contemporary example is the multifaceted engagement and cooperation of the CSI with other Christian missions and organizations. The cooperation of the CSI and CNI with the Indian Missionary Society (IMS) is one such example. IMS missionaries and evangelists are ordained in the CNI and CSI churches. The IMS, on its part, hands over well-developed mission centres to CNI and CSI

---

[42] Kumar, "Ecumenical Cooperation of the Missions in Karnataka (India) 1834-1989", 112.
[43] Firth, *An Introduction to Indian Church History*, 237.

dioceses in places such as Gujarat, Orissa and West Bengal.⁴⁴ Another example involves the CSI's ongoing mission cooperation with the Evangelical Mission in Solidarity (EMS). The EMS is a community of churches and mission societies in Africa, Asia, Europe and the Middle East. It is a forum that invites project holders from various countries and contexts to share their experiences for mutual learning to effectively pool resources, ideas and methods for strengthening the projects. Thus, it provides an avenue for the mutual exchange of experiences and ideas and for learning from each other. The CSI's involvement with the EMS has been an experience of effective service worldwide through the Project Networking Forum.⁴⁵ Another forum where the CSI stands in mission cooperation is with the Members Mission Forum (MMF) of the Council of World Mission (CWM). The MMF is a platform where representatives from member churches contribute ideas and insights to shape the missional direction of CWM. In this forum, members of the CSI, the CNI and the Presbyterian Church of India (PCI) are active participants in mobilizing and facilitating member churches to engage with God's mission in the light of socio-political issues in society.⁴⁶ On an ecclesiastical level, the CSI Global Ecumenical Partnership meeting in October 2014 is an example of the ongoing cooperation in India. It was represented by twenty-six partner churches and organizations worldwide. This meeting inspired the churches to engage more vigorously in the mission towards reconciliation, justice, peace and life in fullness for all.⁴⁷

Similarly, the Syrian Orthodox Church (SOC) has a growing ecumenical relationship with other churches. It maintains a healthy relationship with other churches and opens the door to students of other denominations to study in its theological seminary. It also initiates cooperation with the independent Syrian churches. Further, SOC maintains active participation in ecumenical bodies such as the World Council Churches (WCC), NCCI and Evangelical associations, which shows SOC's openness with various ecumenical bodies and institutions.⁴⁸ The Mar Thoma Church has developed a close relationship with the Anglican Church. The concordat signed in 1961 maintains a deep relationship at the pastoral and ecclesial levels. The Mar Thoma Church also maintains a relationship with ecumenical bodies such as the WCC, the Bible Society, the National Missionary Society, the Christian Literature Society, the Church's Auxiliary for Social Action, the Young Men's Christian Association, the Ecumenical Church Loan Fund and the Christian Agency for Rural

---

⁴⁴ Mark Oxbrow and Emma Garrow eds, *Emerging Mission: CMS/IEM Report* (London/Bangalore/Delhi: CMS/IEM/ISPCK, 2005), 11-12.
⁴⁵ Solomon Paul, "Evangelical Mission in Solidarity Initiates Projects Networking Forum Between its Projects Holders," in *CSI Life* 15:5 (May 2017), 2.
⁴⁶ K. James Cecil Victor, "CSI At South Asia Region Members Mission Forum," in *CSI Life* 15:5 (May 2017), 28.
⁴⁷ "Global Ecumenical Partners Meet: A Brief Report," *CSI Life,* 12:11 (November 2014), 12-13.
⁴⁸ Adai Jacob, "The Jacobite Syrian Orthodox Church: Identity, Challenges and Problems Today," in *Jeevadhara* 34:202 (2004), 289.

Development, by lending the services of its personnel as and when the need arises.[49]

Pentecostal churches in India are also gradually finding their place towards fuller cooperation with other traditional churches through involvement in ecumenical organisations and bilateral relationships. The Pentecostal Mission Church (PMC) became a member of the WCC in 1961.[50] A number of Pentecostal theological seminaries such as the Faith Theological Seminary, Kerala, the India Bible College and Seminary, Kerala, and the New Theological College, Dehradun, are built on convictions of ecumenical cooperation. The acceptance and offering of the Senate of Serampore College syllabuses is indicative of the ecumenical spirit of these institutions. They also keep a tri-polar view, namely: Ecumenical, Evangelical and Pentecostal or Charismatic. Admitting students from different denominations and training them under the umbrella of the Senate of Serampore College as well as the Asia Theological Association shows both the "ecumenical openness" and Evangelical understanding of these colleges. They also accommodate teachers from different churches such as Methodist, Baptist, Presbyterian, Pentecostal and even from Roman Catholic backgrounds. Thus, these Pentecostal colleges can be considered as examples of institutions open to ecumenical ventures.

At the institutional level, the Asia Theological Association currently has 326 member institutions from 33 nations across Asia, South Pacific, West Asia, Europe and the United States.[51] The Senate of Serampore College has 71 affiliated colleges all over India.

In the medical field, the Christian Medical Association of India (CMAI) and Emmanuel Hospital Association (EHA) are based on the fellowship of various Christian hospitals in India. The CMAI is a fellowship of 270 institutional members making a significant contribution to academics, healthcare, development and other relevant issues through a Christian perspective. The Emmanuel Hospital Association (EHA) is another fellowship of Christian hospitals in North India. EHA became a reality with the cooperation of missionaries from the UK, USA and Australia. It currently has a membership of twenty hospitals and forty-two projects covering twelve states of North, Northeast and Central India.

In the twenty-first century, sincere efforts have been made by the NCCI, the Evangelical Fellowship of India and the Catholic Bishops Conference of India towards mission cooperation to strengthen the churches against Hindu fanaticism and the increasing persecution of minority communities in India. In July 2012, Christians joined Hindus, Sikhs, Buddhists and Muslims, to form a united minority front in Bangalore to challenge the communal politics in India.[52]

---

[49] M.J. Joseph, "The Mar Thoma Church: Historical Heritage and Challenges," in *Jeevadhara* 34:202 (July 2004), 318-319.
[50] Marta Palma, "A Pentecostal Church in the Ecumenical Movement," in *The Ecumenical Review* 37:2 (April 1985), 223.
[51] "Membership", accessed October 2021, https://www.ataasia.com/membership/.
[52] Siga Arles, "Relationship Between Ecumenicals and Evangelicals in Asia," in *History of Ecumenical Movement: Issues, Challenges and* Perspectives, comp. Watimongla Jamir (Kolkata: Sceptre, 2014), 229.

Shifts in Mission Cooperation: A Legacy of Ecumenical Movement

The Indian Church Union movement is a model of cooperation between churches worldwide. It has influenced similar movements in many countries resulting in the emergence of the United Churches of Australia, the United Churches in the continent of Southern and West Africa, the United Churches in the island nation of Jamaica in the Caribbean, the United Churches in Canada and the United Church in Pakistan. Of course, each of these united Churches, emerging in the second half of the twentieth century, had its distinct emphasis and vision of unity and priority for mission.[53] Nevertheless, the mission cooperation movement, which began in India, influenced churches in many countries worldwide.

Mission Cooperation: Problems and Prospects in the Contemporary India Context

K.M. George opines that most of the recommendations of consultations and commissions on mission cooperation remain only on paper. The inner life of the churches, either mainline or independent, evangelicals or liberals, derails the effort towards united witness in pluralistic religious Indian society.[54] Even in cases where unions of churches were successful, problems still exist. In the initial period of life in a union, the church concentrated on strengthening the dioceses and uniting different congregational patterns into one. This tended to increase disunity. The basic source of disunity in the Indian Church is and has been communalism. Bengt Sundkler argues that the church union was based on the strength and social significance of communal ties, which not only made denominational differences almost irrelevant in the life of the Indian Christian community, but drew them together across denominational lines. It meant that although denominational differences were overcome whenever a church union was formed, communal divisions persisted in the churches.[55] Churches were able to surmount the superficial decisive forces but not the basic decisive force in the life of the churches. Let us look into the decisive forces that continue to weaken the codes of unity in the Indian churches:

First, corruption, nepotism and power play: The epidemic of societal corruption seems to have taken root in almost all sections of the church. It is a common knowledge that corruption exists in most of the institutions run by the

---

[53] Masilamani Azariah, *Dream and Reality: CSI After 60 Years* (Madras: CSI Diocese of Madras, n.d.) 12.
[54] George, *Church of South India*, 256; *Oikomene Church Union: A Call for Re-Examination*, Comp. J. Paul Sudhakar et al (Madras: C. S. I., n.d.), 233-234.
[55] *Ibid.* 242.

CSI,[56] CNI,[57] Mar Thoma,[58] Tamil Evangelical Lutheran Church,[59] Evangelical Churches of India[60] and Pentecostal churches (especially institutions run by individuals), and that most of the appointments in such church-owned educational, medical and developmental institutions, as well as the selection of contractors and managers involve underhand dealings, bribery and nepotism. In the churches, relatives and friends of powerful group are preferred for positions of power and influence at the expense of others who could well be more qualified and experienced. The churches are turned into "job" banks. In many churches, the clergy hold powerful positions and are not accountable to anybody in the parish.[61] A bishop's election has become a serious issue because large amounts of money are spent on elections.[62] Devoid of any Christian principles, power politics has crept into church life. Canvassing, cajoling, promises of favour and so on, have become the order of the day.

Second, property disputes and court cases: One of the curses that has befallen the churches in India today is that of endless property disputes and the resulting court cases. Property disputes between groups within a church or denomination have rocked the unity of the Indian Church. Many parishes and dioceses are plagued by a variety of unnecessary litigations and agitations that poison the church life. Many run to the court on the least pretext undermining the church's authority and constitution.[63] The church has to look to the world for justice, whereas God meant it to be the other way round.

Third, economic disparity: There is wide economic disparity between the urban and rural dioceses. The blatant inequalities between the rich and the poor dioceses certainly do not speak well of fellowship and unity in the church. Mutual concerns for the poor have almost vanished in the mission of the church. The prevalence of wide economic disparity reveals the underlying presence of disunity despite ongoing cooperation in the church.[64]

Fourth, Casteism and Parochialism: The unity in the churches and denominations is often marred by casteism and parochialism. The evil of

---

[56] Azariah, *Dream and Reality*, 30.
[57] "Donations to churches in corrupt hands", https://www.indiafaith.in/Encyc/2022/9/30/Donations-to-churches-in-corrupt-hands.html; "EOW arrests bishop P.C. Singh in misappropriation of funds: case recovers Rs 202 crores",https://www.opindia.com/2022/09/eow-arrests-bishop-pc-singh-in-misappropriation-of-funds-case-recovers-rs-2-02-crores-fd-174-bank-accounts/
[58] Alexander Mar Thoma Metropolitan, *The Marthoma Church: Heritage and Mission* (Tiruvalla: Christava Sahitya Samithi, 2016), 129-132.
[59] "Lutheran Church bishop accused of luring people to convert for government job", accessed April 16 2023, https://hindupost.in/dharma-religion/lutheran-church-bishop-accused-of-luring-people-to-convert-for-government-job/.
[60] C. Thanga Kumar, "The Contribution of Evangelical Church of India Towards Theological Education with Special Reference to Allahabad Bible Seminary (Master of Theology Thesis, Senate of Serampore College, 2014).
[61] George, *Church of South India*, 257.
[62] *Ibid.* 255.
[63] George, *Church of South India*, 12-14.
[64] *Ibid.*

casteism has militated the unity in the Indian churches.[65] The so-called high-caste Christians refuse to sit in the same pew and have fellowship with the so-called Dalit or "untouchable" Christians.[66] This evil of casteism and parochialism works against the organic union of the church.

The IMC and Cooperation of Indian Churches: A Mutual Interaction

Western Christian missions entered India with a divided agenda, presenting Christianity often with contradictory claims, which negatively affected mission activities in the region. Amidst the confusion and contradiction, different denominational missions in India began to think about cooperation. Unsolved problems and challenges in the mission field inspired missionaries and Indian Christians to realize that united they would stand and divided they would fall. This resulted in the mission cooperation movement among various churches and missions, bringing a sense of togetherness among the missionaries and native Christians. It provided a sense of unity despite conflicting views in theology and church polity, for the common cause of evangelism, justice and peace.

The IMC provided further impetus towards mission cooperation worldwide, including in India, making the progressive shift towards greater ecumenism possible. It became the stepping stone for cooperation among the various missions and their councils in India. It has facilitated unity among Christian missions in India through common consultation. The IMC Tambaram in particular united the churches not just at the global level but also influenced the younger churches at the local level in regions such as India by focusing on the environment of church and on cooperation and unity. Thus, the IMC and the movement of mission cooperation in India have been foundational in encouraging ecumenical thinking and praxis in the region.

In the present context, mission cooperation continues to significantly contribute to uniting various missions and churches together for fellowship and mission in India. However, its warmth seems to be felt more on paper than in the lived-out life of Indian churches. Vices such as corruption, power play, economic disparities, casteism and property disputes have weakened the spirit of cooperation in the Indian churches. With the rise of religious fundamentalism in India, the need of the hour demands praxis-oriented cooperation through improving the interchurch caring relationship in India to better face contemporary mission challenges.

---

[65] Azariah, *Dream and Reality*, 15; *Oikomene Church Union*, 15.
[66] George, *Church of South India*, 256-257.

The Indian Christian Predicament: Mapping the Reception of the Christian Unity and Mission Cooperation in India's Contextual Realities and Beyond

Kaholi Zhimomi

The denominational diversities in Indian Christian history emerged after the arrival of Western colonizers and missionaries from the sixteenth century onward. Churches and mission centres took their form according to the traditions of the missionaries and mission societies, leading to denominational division among the Indian Christians. However, the missionary zeal in the nineteenth century opened new possibilities for dedicated common goals in the mission fields leading to the establishment of missionary unions and conferences for joint efforts in mission propagation and cooperation. Several regional and national conferences provided space for mutual understanding and Christian commitment. While the union movements and conferences brought together the missionaries and mission agencies, Indian Christians, on the other hand, were moving towards the search for an Indian church, an awareness which developed in the context of the Indian Renaissance, nationalism, the freedom struggle and the Indian Christians' search for autonomy. Indian Christians envisioned an indigenous Indian Christian community free from Western denominationalism and mission allegiance. Ecumenism in India, therefore, was a protest initiated against the imported patterns of denominational fragmentation and missionary paternalism. However, the whole movement of the Indian indigenous church was taken over by the missionary agencies, resulting in the ecumenical movement becoming more orientated towards mission challenges, modification of mission policies and inter-mission relations. The 1910 World Missionary Conference held in Edinburgh attempted to provide continuity to the ecumenical process. In 1912, John R. Mott visited India on behalf of the Edinburgh Conference and strengthened and widened mission cooperation in India. Furthermore, the Tambaram International Missionary Conference in 1938 became a milestone in the ecumenical movement in India, affirming the need for a more visible and organic union.

However, it should be noted that the reception of world Christian unity and mission cooperation was met with contempt as well as misunderstood in India both by the Indian Christians as well as people of other faiths. While the world Christian community was ushering in the first World Missionary Conference at Edinburgh and the subsequent continuation committee, India was demanding national freedom and self-determination from the European colonizers. Christian mission, coming from the lands of the colonizers in India, was viewed with suspicion. Consequently, some of the questions that were raised were: why was there the urgent need for unity among Christians at the beginning of the twentieth century? did the world political turnover at the beginning of the twentieth century lead to the urgency for Christian unity? Did Christianity denationalize the Asian people? Questions such as these cornered the newly converted Indian Christians, especially in their attempt to map their identities within the realities of Indian nationalism and their Christian faith, and this predicament continues in India even today.

The Hindu Suspicion on Ecumenical Movements and Christian Unity

In India, Christian efforts towards unity and cooperation have been viewed with suspicion and seen as an international conspiracy to Christianize the whole world by the Hindu critics. Sapre stated that missionary activities in India have "their roots spread on an international level and behind these, there is a global scheme at work." He quoted Shri J.C. Kumarappa to further his views on the Western missions in India- "The Western nations have four arms: 1. The Army, 2. The Navy. 3. The Air Force and 4. The Church." He held the view that while the first three wings were explicit, the church was not- a view that echoed Stalin, who had named the church "the invisible army." Sapre further believed that the policy of the British Government was to encourage missionary activities in India. However, western imperialism had to face revolutionary activities in several Asian countries in the twentieth century as well as the religious awakening in India during the last decades of the nineteenth century. This challenge to the European powers, according to Sapre, stirred Christian missionary organizations to seek a modus operandi, and thus was born the Ecumenical Movement. He noted that before the commencement of the World Missionary Conference, the All-India Decennial Meet at Madras on September 11-18, 1902, instructed every missionary society to make relentless efforts to Christianize the whole of its mission field.[1] Brahmachari Vishwanathji observed that the foreign-dominated religious organizations, particularly the Christian missionaries, took advantage of the religious freedom in India with "alacrity and announced their plan to convert India into a Christ's land through means fair or foul." He accused the church propagandists of using the mission models of Christian monopolizing, eradication of Indian social cultures such as casteism and communalism, institutionalized education, propagation of Christian theologies and philosophies through theological seminaries and colleges, medical missions and the establishments of charitable and social welfare works. Though he was overtly critical of the foreign plot in India, he did not deny that many Indian Christians were also patriotic. He stated, "Like followers of other faiths, the Christians, in general, are peace-loving, tolerant and non-aggressive. They do not insist that conversion is their bounden duty to God. It is the foreign-controlled religious organizations which play this mischief and try to arouse communal tensions for their own ulterior motives." According to many religious Hindus, the Christian mission and the move towards ecumenical collaboration and unity was a tool to

---

[1] Sapre, "The Background of Global Movement for Christian Unity," in *Vivekananda Kendra Patrika: Distinctive Cultural Magazine of India* 8:2, ed. Eknath Ranade (August 1979), 54-55.

create a Western Christian empire altogether. Mahatma Gandhi also accused the Christian mission in India of denationalizing and europeanising the Indians.[2]

The Indian Christian Struggles Then: Debate over Nationalism and Christian Loyalty

Moving away from the paternalism of the missionaries and their mission agencies was a challenge for the converted Indian Christians as they found themselves in between Indian nationalism and the collapse of the Indian churches. Additionally, they were critiqued by their Hindu counterparts for their dependence on those who colonized them. Indian Christians were judged and labelled anti-Indians for being part of a worldwide movement of ecumenical Christianity funded, directed and governed by Western agencies. During these perilous times, Indian churches were yet to frame their theologies, ecclesiastical forms and institutions and thus were ill-equipped to counter-react to those who critiqued them at the national level.

However, despite the continuous onslaught on Indian Christians, it is a historical fact that the efforts for the Indian church began way back in the latter half of the nineteenth century when the Nadar Christians, around 1858, broke away from the Church Missionary Society and formed the Hindu Church of the Lord Jesus. They tried to indigenize the church and to be a completely self-supporting church without foreign funding. In Bengal too Lal Behari Day agitated against the exclusive missionary control of the church and sought equality for the Indian missionaries and proposed the National Church of Bengal, inclusive of all Christians irrespective of their denominational affiliations.[3] The Bengal Christian Association was formed in 1868 by a group of Christians in Kolkata to aspire for an independent Indian church under the presidency of Krishna Mohan Banerjee.[4] This effort for an Indian church founded on Indian culture and religion was inspired by a spirit of nationalism.

The *Harvest Field*, a well-known missionary journal, first drew attention to the Indian Christians' participation, presence and influence in the initial formation of the Indian National Congress, Madras, in 1887.[5] Missionaries such as Revs. T.E. Slater, C.F. Andrews and E. Greaves were instrumental in urging Indian Christians to participate in politics and join the Indian National Congress. However, the initial spurt of nationalism among Indian Christians faded away by the turn of the twentieth century and their participation in politics declined. Indian Christians were discouraged from attending the meetings of the Indian National Congress by other European missionaries who initially had doubts

---

[2] Brahmachari Vishwanathji, "Need for a Check on the Conversion Activities," in *Vivekananda Kendra Patrika: Distinctive Cultural Magazine of India* 8:2, ed. Eknath Ranade (August 1979), 242-250.
[3] Kaj Baago, *Pioneers of Indigenous Christianity, CISRS & CIS* (Mysore: Wesley Press, 1969), 1-2.
[4] Kaj Baago, "The First Independence Movement Among the Indian Christians," in *Indian Church History Review* 1:1 (June 1967), 65.
[5] *Harvest Field* 8 (February 1888), 278.

about Christian involvement in the majority Hindu political movement. The Indian Christians were also fearful of being labelled as "disloyal" to the Christian missions and the British administration and anxious over the future prospects of life after the independence under the rule of a Hindu majority. Some Christians also remained aloof from the movement to attract "the fat fishes and loaves of the Government."[6] Adding to the dilemma of the Indian Christians, the National Christian Council, the body representing the Protestant churches at the national level, failed to take a definite stand on the nation's struggle for political freedom. Given the context they were in, the Council issued two statements on the political situation in 1917 and 1920. However, according to Kaj Baago, the National Council used "a good number of words, but saying actually nothing." He further remarked, "had the National Council taken a positive stand for political independence, it might have encouraged many more Indian Christians to active participation in the struggle for freedom."[7]

During Gandhi's Non-Cooperation Movement, 1920-1923, Christians in India continued to remain silent spectators except for a few Christian patriots. However, as the nation moved towards a more active appeal for independence, a growing number of educated Indian Christians began to identify themselves with the national movement as well as an effort to form an indigenous church and theology.[8] Eminent among them was V. Chakkarai, who asserted, "if my nationalism and Christianity conflicted I would rather give up my Christianity than my nationalism."[9] Along with him, Indian Christians such as Susil Rudra, S.K. Dutta, K.T. Paul, S. Jesudasan, A.J. Appasamy and V.S. Azariah, under the leadership of a few foreign missionaries such as C.F. Andrews,[10] J.N. Farquhar and Nicol MacNicol initiated the process of developing Christianity in an Indian context envisioning for an Indian national awakening. Nevertheless, with only a few Indian Christians joining in the fight for independence, historical records show the Christians' moral weakness in the national struggle. Many Christians decided to excuse themselves and elected to sit on the fence and watch the national struggle against Britain. They preferred to remain under the program of Westernization and the "mission-compound mentality."[11]

---

[6] G.A. Oddie, "Indian Christians and the National Congress, 1885-1910," in *Indian Church History Review* 2:1 (June 1968), 46-51.
[7] K. Baago, *A History of the National Christian Council of India 1914-1964* (Nagpur: NCCI Christian Council Lodge, n.d.), 28-29.
[8] K.N. Panikkar, *Foundation of New India* (London: Allen & Unwin, 1963), 53.
[9] V. Chakkarai, "Nationalism and Christianity," in *Young Men of India* 43:7 (July 1931), 383.
[10] M.M. Thomas, *Acknowledged Christ of the Indian Renaissance* (Madras: Diocesan Press, 1970), 247-249.
[11] Eddy Asirvatham, *Christianity in the Indian Crucible* (Calcutta: YMCA Publishing House, 1955), 25-28.

Against the Institutional Church and Western Church Campaign: Decolonization and Indianization

Because of the growing nationalism worldwide in the early twentieth century, mission agencies and churches all over the world were called to unite and cooperate in response to the urgent evangelistic task. The united action was for the evangelization of the "unoccupied" areas – unity for the sake of evangelization. In India, the first decade of the twentieth century saw the drawing together of Indian Christians from different denominations. The Fourth All-India Missionary Conference in Madras in 1902 can be considered the first real official ecumenical meeting. It saw the founding of the United Theological College in 1910 and the reorganization of the Serampore College. Following this, a series of church union efforts were made by Indian Christians and, singularly, by John R. Mott. Discussions on cooperation and real unity in the Indian churches were directed towards the united constructive policy for a more effective spread of Christianity.[12] In 1914, the National Missionary Council was established to promote mission unity and cooperation. Concurrently, a series of discussions commenced regarding church union negotiations in South India. Against the milieu of international cooperation and unity and the ecumenical beginnings among the mission agencies and churches in India, the Indian Christians increased their demand for "Home Rule" in the churches. V.Z. Azariah stated in the National Council that "Transfer of responsibilities, responsible self-government, opportunities for self-expression are phrases that have become familiar in politics, and the rising generation of Indian Christians is most eagerly looking forward to similar opportunities in the Church."[13] Following his petition, the Council, in 1920, shifted their focus from mission to church, and to the Indian leadership rather than to the missionaries. There was a paradigm shift in missionary work which would later become eminent in the International Missionary Council. In his observation of the world evangelistic movement, J.H. Oldham opined that "If the Church in the mission field is to fulfil its promise and become the chief factor in evangelization it is essential that it should become indigenous."[14]

By the 1930s, there was considerable momentum in the national movement under the leadership of Gandhi, whereas the Indian Christians under the leadership of the National Council, "neither identified itself with nor disassociated itself from the struggle for political independence ... no wonder that the Christian community by and large was considered a foreign-controlled body."[15] The Indian church was also in a dilemma between forming a communal group such as the Muslim League or advocating individual participation in politics. This paved the way for more uncertainties and splits among Indian Christians in the 1920s. By the summer of 1924, there was a representative group meeting to revisit the evangelistic methods of mission and this also started the debate over the issue of proselytization. After vigorous discussions, the Council

---

[12] Sherwood Eddy's Letter to J.E. Tracy, July 25, 1912 (UTC Archives).
[13] Baago, *A History of the National Christian Council of India*, 30.
[14] *Ibid.* 31.
[15] Baago, *A History of the National Christian Council of India*, pp. 37.

declared its stance on cooperation with other religious communities with "love and truth" and that Christians should carry out "evangelism in deed[s]," that is, with social service.[16] To foster cooperation with people of other faiths, the Henry Martyn Institute of Islamic Studies was established in 1930, and the institute was considered "in a very real sense a child of the National Christian Council." Christian mission was no longer of the organized church but cooperation in the universal establishment of the Kingdom of God in all human spheres. This inaugurated the Social Gospel Movement, which was later replaced by the Rethinking Mission in 1932. With the new shift in the historical mission framework, there was a move to indigenize the Council and the Indian churches. Oldham's concept of becoming indigenous in the subsequent decades led to the demand for the devolution of missions and the self-governance of the church as well as the integration of church and mission. The Tambaram Conference added a theological background to the demand that the church be kept at the centre. It also emphasized the importance of an indigenous ministry of the church. This would need unity and cooperation among the churches, especially at regional levels. However, the ground reality was that the Indian church and its mission were not integrated, and leadership was still in the hands of its European secretaries.

Following this paradigm shift in mission goals, Christians in India became enthusiastically involved in the evangelistic work of the church in the 1920s and the 1930s, led by the Evangelistic Forward Movement and the Forward Movement in Evangelism. However, this evangelistic movement received major criticism from opponents of Christian mission both in the West and in India, who accused the missionaries of inducing people to convert through illicit means such as education, financial assistance and so on. Christians also faced accusations from Gandhi for using social, medical, educational and economic upliftment programmes for proselytization and conversion. Answering Gandhi, Christians such as Stanley Jones condemned proselytization but maintained their reason for such social work as a "proclamation of Jesus Christ."[17] This led to the rethinking of whether their primary task was evangelism or social work, and the answer was unanimous: evangelism. Subsequently, there was a rift between Indian Christians and the missionaries since the Indian Christian leaders were apprehensive of the mass movements and evangelistic methods applied by the Forward Movement. But with the turmoil of the Second World War, the missionary leadership as well as the era of the Forward Movement came to an end. Further, with the political development in India, Indian Christians took over the executive and administrative leadership of the National Council.[18]

Because of the Cripps' offer,[19] the Indian National Congress' dissatisfaction with the offer and the subsequent arrest of the Congress leaders, including

---

[16] *Ibid.* 37-47.
[17] John C.B. Webster, "Gandhi and the Christians: Dialogue in the Nationalist Era." In *Hindu-Christian Dialogue: Perspective and Encounters*, ed. Harold Coward (Maryknoll, NY: Orbis, 1989), p. 89.
[18] *Ibid.* 54-60.
[19] In March 1942, the Cripps mission led by Stafford Cripps was dispatched to India with constitutional proposals to gain Indian support for the war effort. Stafford Cripps,

Gandhi, Indo-British relations were strained. This placed the Christian community in a precarious situation, further straining the relationship between Indian Christians and the missionaries. With the National Council finally taking a strong stand in matters of politics and nationalism, Indian Christians were finally clear and firm in their support of the national struggle and their involvement in other political engagements.[20] Ironically after India's independence, Christian minorities faced increased restrictions by radical Hindus which escalated further in the 1950s and subsequent years, due to their historical ties with missionaries.

Ecumenical Ventures in the Twentieth Century

With the initial apprehensions and challenges within and outside the church, the ecumenical ventures in India developed gradually before leaving their mark in the history of the ecumenical movement. The adaptation of denominational affiliations to suit the culture of the mission field resulted in bringing uniformity in missionary activities and teachings. In the twentieth century, ecumenical agencies such as the Christian Literature Society, Christian Endeavour Union, Student Christian Movement in India (SCMI), Indian Missionary Society (IMS), Young Men's Christian Association (YMCA), Young Women's Christian Association (YWCA), Student Volunteer Movement in India, Youth Christian Council for Action and most importantly the National Council of Churches in India (NCCI), provided the pattern for future ecumenical movements, under the leadership of Sherwood Eddy, V.S. Azariah, K.T. Paul, C.J. Lukas, G.V. Job, A.J. Appasamy and V. Santiago. Further, ecumenical institutions such as the Madras Christian College, Tambaram, Women's Christian College, Madras, the United Theological College, Bangalore and the Jaffna College, North Ceylon, functioned as the unifying force.[21] Other union movements such as the Theological Association, the Society for Biblical Studies India (SBSI), the Fellowship of Indian Missiologists (FOIM), the Church History Association of India (CHAI), the Christian Institute for the Study of Religion and Society (CISRS) and the Henry Martyn Institute of Islamic Studies at Hyderabad, played a major role in the proliferation of ecumenical discussions.[22]

The first National Missionary Council (NMC) was held in Kolkata in 1914 (it changed its name to the National Christian Council or NCC, in 1921). For the first nine years, the National Council was a council of missions, not churches. The members were representatives of missionary societies, and consequently,

---

the leader of the House of Commons and a member of the British War Cabinet, was a left-wing Labourite who actively supported the Indian national movement.
[20] Baago, *A History of the National Christian Council of India*, 61-62.
[21] Arun Gopal, "Platinum Jubilee: The Ecumenical Journey of C.S.I.," in *The New Guardian: A Christian Journal of Public Affairs* 4:2 (October 2021), 4. Also see Roger Gaikwad, "Churches Together in God's Mission" in *History of Ecumenical Movement*, comp. Watimongla Jamir (Kolkata: Sceptre, 2014), 214-220.
[22] Jesudas M. Athyal, "The Indian Ecumenical Symphony: Significant Movements and Persons," in *A Light to the Nations*, ed. Jesudas M. Athyal (Geneva: WCC Publications, 2016; New Delhi: ISPCK, 2016), 10.

for the most part, missionaries. Thus, the NCC can be distinguished from the work of the 'Indian Church'. The Council was a fervent supporter of missionary cooperation and church unity in India. Nevertheless, the NCC was a fervent supporter of missionary cooperation and church unity in India. It was, as Baago noted, "the cornerstone of the co-operative edifice in India and the guide to basic inter-mission and inter-church relationships."[23] Regional councils affiliated with the NCC were formed in state or language areas. In 1979, the NCC became the National Council of Churches in India (NCCI), with its headquarters at Nagpur. The NCCI initiated various programs, including those focused on interfaith dialogue, Dalit, Adivasi, Tribal issues, and marginalized communities. It continues to mobilize churches' response to important social and political issues and to address the challenges Christians face in India.[24]

India witnessed ecumenical success in the formation of the Church of South India (CSI) and Church of North India (CNI), which to some extent was the indirect outcome of the missionary cooperation initiated by the National Council, although it never actually initiated bringing the churches together for union negotiations.[25] The union of the episcopal and non-episcopal churches to form the CSI in 1947 and the CNI in 1970 was considered a historic breakthrough in the world's ecumenical history. Jesudas M. Athyal opined that "one of the crucial contributions of India to the ecumenical movement was the assertion that Christian unity needs to be a totalising experience that embraces men and women of all social, ethnic and racial categories."[26]

The emergence of ecumenical study centres facilitated a platform for ecumenical research, interfaith relations, peacebuilding, dialogue, ecological concerns, marginality, cooperation, unity and reconciliation within an ecumenical framework. These centres, unions of churches, colleges and institutions enabled Christians to come together, crossing the boundaries of the denominations and missionary societies. The ecumenical discussions opened enhanced historical research on the process of colonial paternalism and associated issues of Christianity in India. However, in the contemporary context, we recognize that the unending issues concerning ecclesiastical or denominational allegiance and identities undermine the Christian presence in India. Some churches or ecclesiastical hierarchies and institutions tend to identify and work exclusively among a particular group or denomination. This polarization weakens the ecumenical venture in many ways. Even today, ecclesiastical divisions persist in many parts of India. Pentecostal, Charismatic, Revival and Mega Churches are developing and also dividing rapidly. Key challenges to Christian unity in India include racial, caste, tribal, and regional diversity, as well as the need for responsible organizational adjustments and acknowledgment of 'the other'. The church union discussions in India are more

---

[23] Baago, *A History of the National Christian Council of India*, 19-20.
[24] Gaikwad, "Churches Together in God's Mission" in *History of Ecumenical Movement*, 214-220.
[25] Baago, *A History of the National Christian Council of India*, 85.
[26] Athyal, "The Indian Ecumenical Symphony: Significant Movements and Persons," 5-6.

concerned with doctrinal and hierarchical or structural unification. The fundamentalist approach and the authoritarian centralization of the church conflicts with liberal ecumenical theology. A general impression among Christians in India is that ecumenism does not have much dynamism left. We acknowledge the recent halt in the progress towards Christian unity. The talk of church unity has become a platform for power and leadership struggle. Moreover, the ecumenical movement itself is not sufficiently rooted in the life and ministry of the local congregations in India. Therefore, the majority at the grassroots continue to be ignorant of ecumenism and the relevance of ecumenism today. In general, ecumenism remains an issue of interest only for church leaders and theologians.

Trajectories at Hand for Reimaging Ecumenical Vision

At the heart of the ecumenical movement was the impulse for the unity of the church, with an acknowledged appropriate diversity. Konrad Raiser[27] remarked that the ecumenical movement during the 1970s was characterized by a significant widening of scope and agenda that included inter-religious dialogue, racism and ethnicity, science, technology and ecology, the Bible, spirituality, ecumenical formation and women.[28] But there is still an ambivalence about the ecumenical experience in the churches and societies amidst conflicting contexts. Walter Kasper[29] states that the ecumenical movement is today clearly in a transitional period, and ecumenical dialogues have yielded good fruits, but one cannot overlook the theological, political and institutional critique of the movement. He goes on to say that there are two sides to the ecumenical movement at the global level: "On the one side, unions and alliances, a huge number of bilateral and multilateral ecumenical consensus or convergence documents are being observed while on the other side, tensions and even new divisions, often because of ethical questions, are being witnessed."[30] Therefore, for many, ecumenism has become a negative term, equivalent to syncretism, doctrinal relativism and indifferentism. Among other defects, there is a fear of losing one's own Christian identity. From this perspective, what becomes of the present ecumenical ecclesiology response? Across diverse attempts at ecumenical discussions in the recent past, it can be determined that the true vision of ecumenism is yet to be fully achieved. Obviously, this does not mean that ecumenical endeavours *per se* were a complete failure, but the questions that need to be addressed are: Are contemporary ecumenical efforts bound by outdated visions? Is ecumenism limited only to a certain context? How can

---

[27] Konrad Raiser was the General Secretary (1993-2003) of the World Council of Churches.
[28] John Briggs and Mercy Amba Oduyoye, eds. *A History of the Ecumenical Movement, 1968-2000*, Vol. 3 (Geneva: WCC Publication, 2000), xiv.
[29] Walter Kasper was the President of the Pontifical Council for Promoting Church Unity (2001–2010).
[30] "The Ecumenical Movement in the 21st Century", accessed February 22 2023, https://fsspx.news/en/news-events/news/ecumenical-movement-21st-century-cardinal-walter-kasper-21264.

ecumenism be refined in contemporary multiplicities? The call is the depoliticization of ecumenical unity going beyond Christianity and contesting the Christian consciousness by re-examining former methods and working on new models of ecumenism.[31] Confronting these challenges, the church must unite to provide hope for life, eco-human well-being, social justice, and inclusivity for those on the fringes of society, fostering holistic growth. The church might need to consider joining hands with different communities and religions for the service of all, as religions divide, but service unites.[32]

1. Reimagined Christian Cooperation for a Political Mission

The current trend of politics and faith in India is the ongoing majority-minority discourse advocated by the Rashtriya Swayamsevak Sangh (RSS) through its political wing, the Bharatiya Janata Party (BJP). Their agenda of a unified homogeneous India leaves no space for the tolerance of minorities such as Christians, who have been frequently labelled anti-nationals on different occasions.[33] The interplay of politics and faith in India today is a threat to the rights of minorities as faith has been politicized since, with a separatist worldview, there is the negative "othering", demonizing the "other", assimilating the "other" and ostracizing the "other". These metanarratives do not endorse plurality and are aimed at privileging the majority. From this vantage point, can Indian Christians unite for a Christian value-based political ministry or even for church-based activism? Given the history of the NCCI's[34] ambivalent position during the Indian national movement and the subsequent critique by the Hindu nationalists, can the new generation of Christian movements and churches engage in a Christian political mission? In India, dialogue needs to extend to the area of politics. Felix Wilfred opined that all religious groups are political, and therefore, they are consciously or unconsciously part of the political interplay.[35] Rather than staying isolated from politics, the Indian church should collaborate with various organizations and agencies to promote social awareness and combat the issues of religious violence and pseudo-nationalism[36]

---

[31] Kaholi Zhimomi, "Beyond the Serampore Mission Historiography: Re-defining Ecumenism from the Context," in *Serampore Mission Perspectives in Contexts*, ed. Johnson Thomaskutty (Delhi, Pune: ISPCK, UBS, 2019), 264-266.
[32] Gaikwad, "Role of Churches in Nation-Building," 86-87.
[33] K.M. Panikkar, "Outsider as enemy: Politics of rewriting history in India," *ICHR, vol. XXXVI, No.2* (2002), pp. 73-89.
[34] NCCI as in National Christian Council of India since 1921. The acronym NCCI came to represent the National Council of Churches in India in 1979.
[35] Felix Wilfred, *On the Banks of Ganges, Doing Contextual Theology* (Delhi: ISPCK, 2002), 67.
[36] Emmanuel E. James, "The Issues and Challenges Facing Christians in India," in *TBT Journal* 6 (Bangalore: TBT, 2004), 13-14.

2. Reimagining the Church for a Hybrid Ecclesiology

Indian ecclesiology is not one but many ecclesiologies with the presence of major ecclesiological traditions such as the Roman Catholics, the Syrian Orthodox and the Protestants and many more churches that have emerged in the last century, including the proliferation of new generation movements. This inter-ecclesial setting in India demands a unique communion because of the diverse theological, liturgical and spiritual traditions. It calls for a deeper understanding of the church's legitimate diversity as essential for catholicity and unity. Hybrid ecclesiology (taking into account the various theological natures of the church along with the empirical environment such as the context and experiences of the millennials, generation z, the poor, disabled, and people discriminated against based on caste, region, race and gender) should be launched to give space to those otherwise silenced. In India, church union movements have contributed to church politics and power dynamics, so reimagining a traditional ecumenical union of churches will seem superfluous. However, hybrid ecclesiology based on diversity could give a new meaning to mission cooperation and work beyond the boundaries of the church. In hybrid ecclesiology, the people of God can join God's mission no matter what their context might be. Therefore, the traditional churches are challenged to embrace this new methodology in order to engage with a more diversified Indian ecclesiology if they want ecumenicity to work in a diverse Indian ecclesiological context.

3. Reimagining Mission for a Life-Centric Mission

How to retain the quality as well as the fullness of life must be the concern of the ecumenical movement. Because we continue to retain the Church-centric ecumenism, ecumenism remains idealistic even today. We need to move from a Church-centric (concern for the unity of the church) and anthropo-centric (concern for unity and well-being of humanity), to a life-centric ecumenism (concern for the welfare of the whole life on earth). Theology/ies can degenerate into a nationalist, rightist or leftist ideology, and no Christian movements are immune to such tendencies. Therefore, a self-critical theological reflection is imperative for addressing the many issues in the twenty-first century. Ecumenism will reduce itself to a functional presidency if it focuses only on the fundamental campaign. Moreover, insignificant ecumenical theoretical contests deficient of the grassroots, such as women, the poor, the Dalits, the adivasis and the tribal people are deemed futile. For the global or Indian church to establish an ecumenical identity, it must begin by deconstructing entrenched hierarchies and fostering inclusivity for "the other" within society. It should seek not the union of the churches but the union of Christians and human beings and the world.

Towards a Reflective, Transformative and Experiential Ecumenism

Transformative ecumenism challenges the existing social and economic order not primarily on the ecclesiastical orders of hierarchy.[37] The ecumenical movement should engage in collaboration with democratic and socialist civil society groups to promote equitable political decisions and active participation. The church must respond to contemporary challenges through common action, advocacy and building awareness together with people of other faiths and other civil societies. Can Indian Christians or the worldwide Christian communities overcome the inherent binaries of "self and other", and redefine the theology of ecumenism from the perspective of the excluded and the otherized? Can we seek a reflective, transformative and experiential ecumenism today? Centring on this, can Christians committed to ecumenical identity challenge the contemporary discourses on ecumenism? Embodying its true essence, ecumenism, in reality, should test whether the church does not only *preach* the "Universal Church", but *lives as part* of the Church Universal. To act *for* or *with* and *of* the "other" is our renewed challenge for "imagined communities" or "transcultural Christians."[38]

---

[37] Huang Po Ho, "A Paradigm Shift in Theology: A Holistic Redemption to God's Creation," in *Green Theology*, ed. Wati Longchar (Kolkata: Sceptre, 2014), 180.
[38] Kaholi Zhimomi, "Towards a Life-Centered Ecumenism," in *On Nations and the Churches: Ecumenical Responses to Nationalism and Migration: Proceedings of the 20th Academic Consultation of the Societas Oecumenica*, eds. Jelle Creemers and Ulrike Link-Wieczorek (Leipzig: Evangelische Verlagsanstalt, 2020), 199.

The Enhancement the IMC Tambaram 1938 Furnished Towards India's Independence

Ajay Chakraborty

The Tambaram conference of 1938 was one of the much younger assemblies of the International Missionary Council (IMC). Most of the delegates at Tambaram were from the so-called Younger Churches. It was also the first-ever ecumenical conference held in Asia in the twentieth century. The splendid new buildings of the Madras Christian College were dedicated to this auspicious occasion. *The World Mission of the Church* remarks, "It may be said without exaggeration that no more suitable premises could have been found [for this conference] anywhere in the world."[1]

The need of the hour at the time was for the church to turn from its exclusive 'old traditional' nature and adopt an inclusive 'new' or 'young' nature. Hence, the organizers came up with the theme, "Church, Community and State." It was essentially a call to change the church's perspective towards its neighbours of other faith 'community' and their understanding of the 'state'. The major subjects for discussion at Tambaram were divided into five primary themes, (i) *faith* by which the church lives; (ii) *witness*; (iii) *life and work* of the church; (iv) *environment* of the church; and (v) *cooperation and unity*.[2] The discussion at Tambaram reminded the younger churches that we live by "faith" and not by *phirangi*/foreign funds and support. Thus, it may not be wrong to say that they re-installed the three-self-principle[3] among indigenous Christians' missionary doctrine, which detached them from western churches and dominations. It also inculcated a pious love for one's land and called for dedicated patriotism towards one's nation. Thus, responding to the need of the hour, they engaged with patriots of other faiths and raised the need for cooperation and unity for the freedom struggle.

It was expected from the Tambaram conference that the church should do its utmost to be loyal and obedient to the state. "[O]nly in extreme cases of consciousness," noted the *Addresses and Other Records*, "when the orders of the state are clearly contrary to the will of God should there be disobedience. This was the attitude of both St. Peter and St. Paul to the empires of their day."[4] Next, the church must do its best to act as the conscience of the state, which should happen in two ways. First, it should "arouse the State to take action, as the representative of the community, against social evils." Secondly, in extreme

---

[1] *The World Mission of the Church* (London: International Missionary Council, 1938), 6.
[2] *Ibid.* 7-8.
[3] Hans-Ruedi Weber, *Asia and The Ecumenical Movement 1895-1961* (London: SCM Press Ltd.), 161.
[4] *Addresses and Other Records, The Madras Series*, Vol. VII (London: IMC, 1939), 107.

cases, the church "may have to criticize, to oppose and to resist the policy and the action of the State."[5] The Indian church faced a significant dilemma in deciding how to respond to British rule in India: what should the attitude of Indian Christians towards India's struggle against colonial power be? Should they participate in a movement that could send back those who had shared the Gospel and had enlightened the colonized community? The dilemma before Indian Christians (and others of the then-western colonies) was tremendous and answers needed to be sought out at Tambaram. This paralleled the situation in Asian churches at the time, where they grappled with the decision of whether the "Eastern Younger churches" should align themselves with the "Western Old churches".

The Tambaram conference largely revolved around the view of one man, Hendrik Kraemer, who had published a book as a study document for the conference: *The Christian Message in a Non-Christian World.* He perceived the danger of compromising the Christian message relating to other religious traditions and ideologies, which he saw manifest in some then-current trends in mission thinking and practice.[6] His book triggered an intense discussion in the build-up to and during the conference. Some in India came out very strongly against Kraemer's view. Did the Tambaram conference compromise the faith? If so, how and why? What does it say about the impact of the socio-political situation of the time on mission thinking? Hence, this contribution attempts to bring to light how the Tambaram conference transformed the mission-oriented leaders in India into nationalist or pro-independence leaders.

It all began in the second half of the nineteenth century when in Bengal, a group of Christians, under Kali Charan Bannerji, formed the *Christo Samaj* (Society of Christ) in 1887 to form a United Indian Church by eliminating Western denominationalism. Bannerji was also active in the Indian nationalist movement with the Indian National Congress (INC). T.V. Philip writes that the ecumenical movement in India "was born under the influence of Indian nationalism at the initiative of Indian Christians."[7] It came as a movement of liberation, the liberation of the churches from the ecclesiastical, cultural and theological colonialism of the West, and aimed at the manifestation of a truly Indian or Chinese or Japanese Christianity. However, the efforts of Indian Christians to form an indigenous church in India did not materialize due to the opposition of the missionaries during Bannerji's lifetime (till 1906). Nevertheless, the nationalist and ecumenical spirit did not completely die out in India[8] and was given a renewed vigour through discussions at the 1910 Edinburgh conference and later the 1938 Tambaram conference.

---

[5] *Ibid*. 108-109.
[6] "Mission and dialogue 50 years after Tambaram", accessed August 25 2021, https://www.religion-online.org/article/mission-and-dialogue-50-years-after-tambram/.
[7] T.V. Philip, *Ecumenism in Asia* (India: ISPCK& CSS, 1994), 144.
[8] Mathews George Chunakara, "A survey of the Ecumenical Scenario in Asia: Prospects and challenges," in *CTC Bulletin* 22:2 (August 2006), 64.

The National Missionary Council (NMC) which was formed in 1914,[9] managed to draw together all the old traditional Protestant denominations of Indian Christianity – Anglicans, Lutherans, Congregationalists and Presbyterians. It formed an advisory committee, which incidentally comprised of only foreign missionaries. Thus, in relation to the political movement in India, the NMC was a little timid.[10] The NMC had ample opportunity through which it could have approached nationalism from a positive perspective. The Indian national struggle of 1905-1934 can be divided into three great waves of nationalism: 1905-10, 1917-22 and 1930-34. The first wave of nationalism was the factor behind the formation of NMC. The second wave influenced the reorganization of the Council in 1923. If these waves impacted the NMC, then the question arises of the NMC's attitude towards nationalism. As Kaj Baago puts it, "Would it cooperate with the nationalists and work for Indian independence? Or would it oppose the struggle for *Swaraj*?"[11] He answered, "neither-nor."[12] Hence, it can be concluded that, at this point, the NMC lacked the courage to join Indian politics.

Why did the Indian Christian community not devote itself to the nationalist spirit? G.V. Job argues that except for the Syrian Christian community, the Indian Christians at the time were very young and needed time to grow into a homogeneous group even within each linguistic area and that the majority of its membership was drawn from the educationally and socially underprivileged ranks of Hindu society.[13] Because of their lowly state, none were willing to give any support to the political movement in India at the time. Another issue was the fragmentation in the Indian Christian community. In the 1930 *NCC Review,* a comment was passed that "our own unhappy division make it impossible for us to offer"[14] towards national politics. Baago writes, "It must be admitted, therefore, that the NCCI hardly lived up to the first word in its name at that time, particularly not when we consider what the word 'National' stood for in those

---

[9] Between December 18-21 1912, during the All-India Missionary Conference held in Calcutta, a proposal to establish the NMC was put forward by 58 delegates from across India who had convened at the Asiatic Society. The inaugural meeting of the NMC took place at the Calcutta YWCA building in February 1914. Kaj Baago, *A History of the National Christian Council of India* (Madras: CLS, 1965), 14-15.
[10] Kaj Baago says, "It too became like gross missionary imperialism. Instead of taking the Indian Church to the right path the members left the Indian Church for itself, because for them Mission and Church were two different entities. After Mission work ends, the NMC will be dissolve. Because of its ability, tact and impartiality in handling the Comity and Co-operation issues, the Council had won the respect and confidence of all parties and established themselves in the Indian Church as well as of the Government, who were making use of the Council. Thus, from merely a consultative and advisory body; it had gained a position of authority and power." Baago, *A History of the National Christian Council of India*, 13.
[11] Realising that they would have to express an opinion, the Council issued two statements on the political situation in 1917 and in 1920, which were ambiguous in their meaning. Baago says, the statements could be interpreted both ways.
[12] Baago, *A History of the National Christian Council of India*, 28.
[13] G.V. Job, *Rethinking Christianity in India* (Madras: Hogarth Press, 1939), 11.
[14] Quoted in Baago, *A History of the National Christian Council of India*, 37-38.

years."[15] The reality was that the Christian community was divided and had no time to devote to national issues.

It was also observed that when Indian Christians desired to attempt something of their own in the way of a new denomination, they found the field already choked with foreign ones. For instance, when the effort towards the South Indian Union of Churches was made, many obstacles were put in the way by Western missionaries' dividing patterns.[16] Another dominating factor was language. The large cities had "English" congregations composed of Anglo-Indians, Europeans and a handful of Indian Christians.[17] Indian languages and indigenous sentiments were rare among the cathedrals in urban centres, which were the decision-makers. Indian Christians, though growing in number, were marginalized by English-speaking people, and could not make the fullest use of the stimulus of Indian nationalism. The division of hierarchy was felt more in English-speaking-dominated congregations. In light of this, J.H. Oldham had two suggestions: First, for Indian Christians to get into church leadership, and second, for the church to relate itself to the new political situation in India. He also proposed to change the name of the Council into an indigenous name. Except for the second plan, the other proposals were accepted. In 1923, the name of the Council was changed to the National Christian Council of India, Burma and Ceylon.[18]

In 1939, the *Rethinking Christianity in India*, through its various articles authored by Indian Christian leaders, reminded Indian Christians of various concerns of the time. One important reminder was that the missionaries' hard work has brought two new ferments and stimuli amongst Hindus to safeguard their religious issue: "one progressive, critical and reformist, and the other conservative and defensive."[19] A similar stimulus can be observed amongst Indian Christians regarding the nationalist issue: on the one hand, a handful of Indian Christians wanted to throw themselves into the fight against British Imperialism; on the other hand, a large number of their friends wanted to remain faithful towards the British missionary enterprise, which had brought the liberating Gospel of Jesus Christ from the same land. Hence, the question arises here, why was it so? While hunting for answers, one must remember that all three major religious groups had local, regional and national concerns during this century. From the beginning of the twentieth century, Hinduism developed a "new nationalism which awakened a sense of jealous pride in everything Indian, and an eager readiness to sacrifice all, even Hindu orthodoxy or religion itself, if necessary, on the altar of political emancipation."[20] Social justice, a concern of the missionary societies in Indian society, appeared as a relatively mild and insufficiently assertive demand when compared to the political motives of the Hindu intelligentsia. The Muslims, who were the next largest community, were oscillating between radical nationalism, which drove some of their members to

---

[15] *Ibid.* 37.
[16] Job, *Rethinking Christianity in India*, p. 13.
[17] *Ibid.*
[18] Baago, *A History of the National Christian Council of India*, 31-33.
[19] Job, *Rethinking Christianity in India*, 4.
[20] Job, *Rethinking Christianity in India*, p. 5.

the side of the Indian National Congress, and communalism. Whenever these two groups snatched some benefits from the British government, the thin bond of nationalism that bound them together would crack and the communal, economic and political rivalry, would be expressed in religious disturbances. For them, the Indian Christian community was unfortunately regarded as the other branch of Western imperialism. In a sense, they weren't wrong. Instead of joining the national cause, Indian Christians, on Christmas day, 1905, at meeting of church leaders held in the historic library of William Carey at Serampore, decided to form the National Missionary Society of India (NMSI) under the leadership of V.S. Azariah with the following principles: (i) the work of evangelization shall be done by Indians; (ii) its expenses should be met with Indian money; (iii) they must choose mission fields in areas where Western missions were not working; (iv) the society should not form a church or denomination but entrust the converts they gather to the care of the churches in that area.[21] This could be interpreted as an indifferent attitude among the Indian Christians towards nationalism. To understand its dynamics, one needs to know the concept of nationalism grasped by Indian Christians.

What was Nationalism for Indian Christians?

In 1939, the document *The World Mission of the Church* classified that the then-world had three major types of nationalism: (i) Self-expressive nationalism: which represented the subjugated people's hunger for self-expression, self-respect and self-determination; (ii) Self-satisfied nationalism: nations such as Western Europe and North America described this as their national loyalties; and (iii) Self-assertive nationalism: this type was of the Soviet Union and China and the other emerging communist world powers.[22] Commenting on this, M.A.C. Warren writes, "Nationalism – regardless of types – is a smouldering vision in the minds of men, fire burning in their bones, a yearning, a cluster of convictions deep within their hearts that defies precise and acceptable definition."[23] Nationalism begins with love for the unity of territory, coveted or possessed. This love is then translated into a desire for political independence. This leads to a sense of group superiority. The conviction grows that the nation does not need to identify itself with other nations or with any religion other than that which is indigenous to the group to attain its true significance.[24] Thus, a necessity for political independence arose among colonized nations. Did Indian Christians share such sentiments towards nationalism? The following discussion will bring to light that initially, except for a few Indian Christians, most were not sure that

---

[21] "25 December 1905 formation of the National Missionary Society of India", accessed January 4, 2022, https://nalloorlibrary.com/2017/12/23/25-december-1905-formation-of-the-national-missionary-society-of-india/.

[22] Quoted in M.A.C. Warren, "Nationalism as an International Asset," in *The International Review of Mission* 44 (October, 1955), 387. *Cf.* Eric S. Fife and Arthur F. Glasser, *Mission in Crisis* (USA: Inter Varsity Press, 1961), 42.

[23] Warren, "Nationalism as an International Asset," 387.

[24] Fife and Glasser, *Mission in Crisis*, 44.

they needed freedom. The 1938 Tambaram conference, however, helped them towards more active involvement in the nationalist movement.

Political Freedom

For some Christians, participating in politics was of the devil, and Indian national politics was of the archdevil. Some of them would say that "political subordination and even persecution are a part of the Christian's lot in life ... the Christians should quietly submit to them. Even when the rulers openly pursue an unjust and unrighteous policy, we should regard their actions as a part of God's inscrutable plan."[25] They were preoccupied with avoiding political involvement because they believed such actions might conflict with the British Empire (which they had been taught by the missionaries, was divinely ordained), and the British Government in India (from which they feared losing practical benefits). They reasoned that the British Empire has saved India from anarchy and corruption following the downfall of the Moghul Empire, that it has given them a stable government and a reasonable brand of justice, and that it has provided the country with a network of railways, telegraphs, post-offices, roads, canals and so on. On these grounds, they argued that it was sheer ingratitude to criticize the British government or do anything that might directly or indirectly weaken its hold upon India.[26]

During the Tambaram Conference, many countries were under the "shadow of war or under its fear." Hence

> the churches reflected on their personal and corporate responsibility to bring a peaceful situation to their nations. They felt they were condemned for their lack of faith, courage, disunity and ineffectiveness. In this situation, they recognized that God has given them "unlimited resources of God," and these days were of His opportunity. Their coming together has renewed their courage and deepened their sense of responsibility. They were burdened to seek the spiritual and moral basis for ordering national life and international relations.[27]

Christian leaders felt the divine force of God to bring the right order and the proper relationship of whole humanity from God who makes history. Grubb opines,

> The prophets of the Old Testament denounced nations and rulers for cruelty and inhumanity, for robbery and lies, and their message is applicable today. Patriotism is clearly not enough. The two great commandments of love require that love to God become our supreme loyalty, which must be exemplified in brotherly consideration for the welfare of all men.[28]

Not only were they down in the spirit because of national problems but also because of world problems. They felt that they were called to understand and interpret kingdom duties with the divergent interpretation of what was their sole

---

[25] Eddy Ashirvatham, *Rethinking Christianity in India* (Madras: Hogarth Press, 1939), 290.
[26] Job, *Rethinking Christianity in India*, 290.
[27] Kenneth G. Grubb, *The Church and the State*, Vol. VI (London: IMC, 1939), 247.
[28] *Ibid.* 248.

responsibility as native Christians. For them, "love your neighbour" meant doing justice to their neighbour. Because they felt that injustice drove nations to desperate courses, including war, the Tambaram IMC's statement in 1939 says,

> we condemn the efforts to impose the will of one people upon another by force, and especially the invasion of the recognised territory of one people by the armed forces of another... justice requires the elimination of the domination of one people by another.[29]

It can be observed here that the IMC supported nationalism. Again, the following statement says,

> God has made all peoples of one blood. No race can therefore disregard the rights and interests of other races... The church should exert its influence on the side of all movements working for the full and equal sharing by all races... We call upon churches and individual Christians to do whatever is within their power to help in the solution of the acute and tragic world problem...[30]

A picture was emerging- while the Christian church was not called upon to determine the purely technical aspects of government, Christians should commit themselves to promoting international cooperation.[31] They felt the call for international peace and justice at all levels. Tambaram council made it clear that,

> in situation of open conflict, the maintenance of the Christian standard of righteousness, justice and mercy becomes at once more urgent and more difficult. ... in any given situation the action that seems in line with God's will is the best decision. Moreover, in the very course of war Christians of the conflicting nations and of the whole ecumenical fellowship should pray and strive for peace, not the mere cessation of hostilities, but the establishment of just relationships.[32]

The call was for long-lasting peace and a right relationship. To fulfil this dream, Tambaram says,

> The church can show her solidarity with the local first through the preaching of the Word and the demonstration of its fellowship. Secondly, by the rare opportunity to influence through her teaching institutions or schools. Training in right attitude and right direction. Education for peace is badly needed... The cinema and radio can be very effective... the church should use these facilities in itself as well as oppose their misuse by others.[33]

How to use the churches' multifaceted talents and secular communication and media for the political benefit of society was their call to all Christians. They were also willing to think about socio-cultural and religious aspects of independence from Western powers.

Socio-Cultural, Religious Independence

The British administration offered a religious electorate to Hindus, Muslims and Christians. This was, however, seen as part of their divide-and-rule formula. By

---

[29] *Ibid.*
[30] Grubb, *The Church and the State*, p. 249.
[31] *Ibid.*
[32] *Ibid.* 252.
[33] *Ibid.* 253.

opposing the scheme of the communal electorate, Indian Christians showed that the enlightened Christian conscience could take a more dispassionate view of things and help people keep their heads amidst the perplexities of communal rivalries (though in doing so, they, a minority community, renounced the protection of the scheme).[34] Job comments on these vital issues, "Like St. Paul we are neither circumcised nor uncircumcised but we are new creation. Are we trying to join Hindus and Muslims in this national movement or standing against Western Christians? We are to create New Indians." He advised even the West "to leave cultural traditions alone and turn to the practical task of standing up for Christ's ideals for humanity which are so wantonly being trampled under the feet of rampant nationalism."[35]

It is important to keep in mind here that there were two classes of Indian Christian congregations. There were those who were educated and wealthy and those who remained almost on the level of the most backward classes.[36] Economically and educationally, the advanced sections were found in large cities and towns. Congregations of small towns were employed in mission schools or hospitals. And these two classes, although united in the blood of Christ, were divided by differences in interests. It resulted in a dual response to nationalism. Some Indian Christian apologists were content with the ideology that "Our primary allegiance, they say, is not to the country which gave us *birth* but to the religious community to which we *belong*." Some apprehended that "Nationalism means the assertion of Hindu domination and the re-establishment of caste, idolatry and superstition."[37] They argued that they would lose their so-called Indian Christian culture if *swaraj* became a reality.[38] Encouraging nationalism would devour their non-Indian names, non-Indian music and forms of worship, non-Indian church organizations and non-Indian modes of living. Such fears were not unfounded, as can be seen in the heated controversy in South India at the time when the Congress government enacted a prohibition of sacramental wine in the Communion Service.[39] Thus, Indian Christians were confused about whether it was God's will to join the Hindus and Muslims in the national cause.

Economic Freedom

While many Indian Christians embraced their newfound faith out of religious conviction, others sought material advantages. Among this second group was a large host of secular-minded Christians who urged material consideration in defeating nationalism. In the early years when *swaraj* was still a dream, this group boldly stood for nationalism. However, in the fourth decade of the twentieth century, communism was spreading rapidly among Indian Christians.

---

[34] Job, *Rethinking Christianity In India*, p. 14.
[35] *Ibid.* 24.
[36] *Ibid.* 30.
[37] Ashirvatham, *Rethinking Christianity In India*, p. 290.
[38] The Hindi word *swaraj*, meaning 'self-rule', was popularly used during India's independence movement to refer to freedom from foreign domination.
[39] *Ibid.* 291.

Influenced by communist ideology, they argued that since Indian Christians were a small minority of just two percent of the population, it was wise to join hands with other minorities in getting benefits for themselves. This would help them procure money from the government for schools and scholarships and in securing representation for Indian Christians on bench courts and municipal and district boards.[40] They argued that, given the economic impoverishment of their community, it was imprudent to forgo opportunities for financial gain in favour of national service or imprisonment for one's convictions. Hindus, on the other hand, they argued, could afford to throw away their jobs and even march into jail because of the insurance they had in the form of the joint family system.[41]

The Tambaram 1938 conference indirectly motivated Indian Christians to break free from the state of neutrality, often likened to the immovable Gibralter rock.[42] If the free development of the human spirit was at the very centre of Christianity, then the need of the hour was to see the establishment of a modern India where every individual and group's birth right is stressed.[43] If Christians believed that Mahatma Gandhi's slogan of non-violence was the Christian principle, should they then not join the nationalism of non-violence, which rejected "war to end war"? Some Indian Christians joined the mass movement of freedom struggle, along with their struggle for the church's freedom.

Glimpses of Indian Christian Participation in the National Movement

Azariah gave his balanced opinion that "our young theologians want autonomy at one step; sober minds are willing to work more slowly but legitimate aspirations must be met." He defined this ideology as the independence movement of the Indian church from the hands of the Western missionary societies: "the curtailment of missionary power; the training of Indian leadership in the government of their own church; the preparation of the whole Christian community for indigenous leadership and self-support." He gave a slogan: "Do not fear to take risks. Believe in the Holy Spirit and trust men."[44] In 1939, Eddy Asirvatham wrote,

> Many an Indian Christians is afraid of anything savouring of nationalism, because he has not been properly informed of its meaning. It is true that in the name of nationalism every imaginable sin has been committed. At present moment a raging, tearing kind of nationalism is occupying the foreground in Fascist Italy, Nazi Germany, and Militarist Japan. It is this type of nationalism which Tagore decries when he describes it as "the organized self-interest of a whole people ...[45]

---

[40] *Ibid.* 290-291.
[41] *Ibid.* 292.
[42] *Ibid.* 293.
[43] *Ibid.* 294.
[44] Carol Graham, "The Legacy of V.S. Azariah," in *International Bulletin of Missionary Research* (Brill, 1985), 17; Accessed December 27, 2021, https://journals.sagepub.com/doi/abs/10.1177/239693938500900106.
[45] Ashirvatham, *Rethinking Christianity in India*, 286.

Although different ideologies were among people, he supported the only kind of nationalism that puts into practice the motto,

> live and help others to live ... From the point of view of a Christian, nationalism is simply another name for national self-respect ... A man is not worth his salt if he does not take legitimate pride in the past accomplishments of his country, and does not look forward with buoyant hope to what his country may still accomplish in the future.[46]

The discussion at the Tambaram conference occasioned these assertions by Indian Christians on nationalism. P.D. Devanandan disagreed with the Kraemerian influence at the conference, where "any programme of merely earthly betterment" was rejected. Devanandan argued for a Christian concern in society and desired the creation of a theology that regarded a positive approach to other religions and cultural contexts.[47] He believed that Christian concern in society was not just political or economic but primarily theological, rooted in and governed by the insight that "our faith stands for the redemption of the whole man" here and now.[48]

Along with individual personalities, even the National Christian Council of India (NCCI) changed its ideology towards nationalism. Baago notes three important changes in the identity and role of the NCCI at the beginning of the 1940s. One among them was the attitude of the Council to the nationalist movement, which had so far been somewhat ambiguous. However, in the 1940s, it came out unequivocally in support of the Indian National Congress and its demand for Indian independence.[49] Other Christian bodies followed similar anti-British utterances: Madras Christian Council, Tinnevelly Church leaders, students of the United Theological College, Bangalore and Calcutta church leaders such as S.K. Datta condemned the arrest of the Congress leaders and demanded immediate independence and urged the British churches to develop new policies to alleviate the political tension in India.[50]

Post-independence, Indian Christians continue to advocate the need to engage in nation-building. In his book *Asia and Western Dominance*, K.M. Panicker proposes that people from all walks of life in Asia, regardless of their religious or political affiliations, were deeply determined to break free from imperial rule. However, the connection between Christian missionary efforts and aggressive imperialism brought about political complexities. He asserts that people's national sentiment could not ignore viewing missionary activity as inimical to a

---

[46] Chakkarai, *Rethinking Christianity in India*, 287-288.
[47] Siga Arles, "Mission in the Indian Cultural Context: The significance of Paul David Devanandan," in *Indian Journal of Theology* 56; Accessed December 27, 2021, https://biblicalstudies.org.uk/pdf/ijt/35-2_055.pdf.
[48] P.D. Devanandan, "Report from the Christian Institute for the study of Society," *NCR* (1951), 323.
[49] Baago, *A History of the National Christian Council of India*, 20.
[50] "Christians in India and the Political Situation" *Review* (1942), 437. In 1943, the British Council of Churches responded to this appeal by providing a limited defence and explanation of British policy in India along with the promise to urge for independence for India after the war.

country's interests.[51] This inspired like-minded leaders to courageously champion the cause of resisting imperial power. Another ecumenical Christian leader, M.M. Thomas, collaborated with David McCaughey on a pioneering study titled 'The Christian in the World Struggle.' This study was the first of its kind to provide an ecumenical response to the 'revolutionary changes' stemming from global political upheaval after World War II and the national independence movements in Asia, Africa, and Latin America.[52] This study encouraged Christians to come out of their cocoons and join national and humanitarian causes.

Evaluation and Conclusion

Since the emergence of Indian nationalism, Indian Christians grappled with their stance in the movement. Some chose to actively support the national cause, while others remained detached. As a minority community, Indian Christians found themselves torn between their devotion to 'Jesus' in matters of faith and 'Justice' in secular life. Nevertheless, a courageous few wholeheartedly dedicated themselves to the national cause. Regrettably, due to the self-interest of some Indian Christians, only a handful of patriots committed themselves to the struggle. Meanwhile, other Indian Christians focused on personal gain, while missionary leaders often emphasized a gospel divorced from its social and political implications. Hence, their excuse was that the British Empire was a good government and that it deserved their sympathy. The Empire had come with the "white man's burden," "sacred trust" and "mission of civilization" and so in gratitude Indian Christians would be doing the right thing by rejecting any form of political agitation. They rejected the truth that any nation rules others purely out of selfish motives.

The IMC Tambaram 1938 theme and sub-themes caught Indian Christians' attention. I believe it assisted them in inculcating an ideology of having faith in God and becoming true witnesses amongst others through their life and work by creating an environment of cooperation and unity among themselves and their non-Christian friends. After India gained its political independence from colonial rule, Indian Christians even helped the "younger churches" of India to gain independence from the control of missionary societies. There are similar reports of Tambaram's influence on Christian attitudes towards nationalism in other parts of the world. For example, Thompson Samkange from Zimbabwe, who attended the Tambaram conference, involved himself in the national movement of his country.[53] A Japanese Christian writer Uchimura Kanzo said, "I love two J's and no third; one is Jesus and the other is Japan."[54] Harendra Kumar

---

[51] K. M. Panicker, *Asia and Western Dominance.* London: George Allen & Unwin, 1959.
[52] M.G. Chunakara, "M.M. Thomas' Contributions to the Worldwide Ecumenical Movement" (August, 2015), www.marthoma.in.
[53] Frieder Ludwig, "Mona Hensman: An Indian Woman at the World Missionary Conference in Tambram (1938)," in *The Journal of World Christianity* 6:1 (2016), 124.
[54] Fife and Glasser, *Mission in Crisis*, 54.

Mukherjee, a Bengali Christian, while working with the team to prepare the Indian Constitution, abolished the right of "reservation" for his own Christian community. It can be assumed that he did so because of "National" feelings rather than for building his own community. It would therefore be accurate to say that the IMC Tambaram played a significant role in advancing the journey of Indian Christians towards India's independence and the liberation of Indian churches from Western influence.

II. UNITY, COOPERATION AND DIALOGUE

Proposal for "Informal Dialogue": Christian Witness in the Context of Hindu-Majority India

John Arun Kumar

Since the mid-twentieth century, interreligious dialogue has been "increasingly promoted as a factor helping to secure peace and mitigate conflict on the local, regional, and global level."[1] Around fifty years ago, the World Council of Churches began its interreligious dialogue program with a multi-lateral dialogue in Ajaltoun, which also involved Hindus. Stanley Samartha, a theologian from South India, was the first director of the program. Samartha saw Christian and Hindu thought as compatible in many aspects. However, he faced resistance from both Indian and non-Indian Christians, as they were critical of his pluralist tendencies. From the start, both Christians and Hindus disagreed on the understanding of interreligious dialogue. Currently, as pointed out by Melanie Barbato, the "disagreement about both the desirability and possible formats of Hindu-Christian dialogue continues."[2]

I see that interreligious dialogue has remained generally at formal levels. However, in the current situation in India, it is increasingly challenging to have interreligious dialogue at this level. I suggest that formal engagement is commendable but does not yield any reciprocal interest. Thus, instead of engaging in formal interreligious dialogue alone, the Indian church should consider models of informal formats in organized dialogues and interactions, which include inter-religious conversations and activities happening in the day-to-day lived experiences of people. Though there are also challenges to informal dialogue, especially under the present regime in India, I suggest that there are immense opportunities for Christian witnesses at the informal level. Informal interreligious interactions occur both in rural and urban settings. I hope to explore this for Christian witnesses in the Hindu majority context using a multi-method approach in this paper.

Terms: Witness, Informal Dialogue and Secular Hindus

K.P. Aleaz argues that the word witness is biblical and resonates with the idea of *prama* and *pramana* in Hindu philosophy. A proponent of the Neo-advaitic approach to Christian witness, he suggests that the word "witness" should be used instead of mission or missions, both of which are missing in the Bible.[3] This

---

[1] Melanie Barbato, "Understanding Hindu Christian Relations" accessed August 6, 2021, https://talkabout.iclrs.org/2021/02/28/understanding-hindu-christian-relations/.
[2] Barbato, "Understanding Hindu Christian Relations."
[3] K.P. Aleaz, "Witnessing Christ in the company of Hindus," in *"Give us friends!": An India perspective on one hundred years of mission*, Papers from the 16th Annual Centre

explanation seems helpful, and I have adopted it in this paper. I use the term "Informal dialogue" as a category to refer to terms such as informal conversations, informal talks, informal activities, day-to-day interactions, daily living amidst multicultural communities, etc. I use this term to denote a range of categories that are viewed as holistic. It has both discursive and nondiscursive intra-religious and interreligious interactions as a whole. Here discursive language means the use of words and nondiscursive language means the use of symbols or actions other than words. Hindus are often discussed in scholarship as pluralists. However, I use the term "secular Hindu" as a category here for Hindus adopting secular views. Writing on "Secular Hindu, secular Muslim," Rajeev Bhargava argues that the term

> "secular" should mean not against religion or a simple-minded acceptance of all religions but "opposition to institutionalised religious domination." I say this because in Europe it connoted opposition to the church, a classic instance of intra-religious domination – and in India, rejection of caste or gender hierarchies, repudiation of religious extremism (intra-religious domination), and, in addition, protection of a religious community from the power of another (inter-religious domination). A secular perspective then demands that, in a multi-religious society, a state be designed to impartially reduce inter- and intra-religious domination. Furthermore, it may help people develop a form of respect proper for their own religion and that of others. For this to happen, states should be impartial, rather than be partial to a particular religious community (Hindus or Muslims) or a section thereof (male, upper castes).[4]

Bhargava's suggestion seems to be based on the idea of equality and it captures well the category of secular Hindus, and I adopt this term in this paper.

Interreligious Dialogue and the Church

Bob Robinson states, "There are many situations in India where informal dialogue has long been an established reality made possible and often inevitable by the proximity of neighbours of different faiths."[5] For instance, Atreyee Sen in her ethnographic study sample from Kolkata of Hindu, Muslim and Christian women from slums and lower-class neighbourhoods shows how they meet and debate religious concerns in informal "resting places" (under a tree, in a park bench, at a tea stall, on a train, at a corner of a railway platform).[6] In her study,

---

for Mission Studies Consultation, UBS, Pune, Annual Centre for Mission Studies Consultation, ed. Frampton F. Fox (Bangalore: CMS / ATC, Asian Trading Corporation, 2010), 80.
[4] Rajeev Bhargava, "Secular Hindu, secular Muslim" (April 15, 2018), https://www.thehindu.com/opinion/op-ed/secular-hindu-secular-muslim/article23543441.ece.
[5] Quoted in Atul Aghamkar, "Hindu-Christian Dialogue in India," in *EAST MEETS EAST: In the Heartland of Hinduism Evangelical Interfaith Dialogue* 2:2 (2011), accessed October 8, 2021, https://fullerstudio.fuller.edu/featured-article-hindu-christian-dialogue-in-india/.
[6] Atreyee Sen, "Gods, Gurus, Prophets and the Poor: Exploring Informal, Interfaith Exchanges among Working Class Female Workers in an Indian City," *Religion* 10:9 (2019), p.2.

she shows that informal inter-religious discussions and shared understandings of gendered oppressions determine the contours of conversational cultures developed by urban working-class women.[7] Here we see informal "resting places" act as safe havens for women from different faiths in slums and lower-class neighbourhoods, working in cities, having informal interfaith discussions and debating religious concerns. Informal places provide natural safe spaces for people to discuss many issues that concern them based on shared humanity.

Referring to Robinson's suggestions, Atul Aghamkar recounts the history of the different types of missionary attitudes in the Hindu-Christian interactions and writes that,

> On the one side, most early missionaries (in the eighteenth and nineteenth centuries), who were largely products of the Pietistic movement, looked at the native religions as sinful, if not Satanic. Hence, their approach to them was more condemnatory. In contrast, particularly in the middle of the twentieth century, a more sympathetic and positive attitude emerged among the Christian missionaries – some of whom even abandoned their missionary vocation and absorbed many religious precepts and practices of the native religions into their own faith. This often led to syncretistic religious practices. However, a large segment of the Christian community in India probably is more inclined to live harmoniously with the people of other faiths, often entering into what we call "informal dialogue" over many central issues of faith and practices.[8]

Aghamkar further suggests that though "informal dialogue is part and parcel of their day-to-day life" in India, it "has not been taken seriously either by the theologians or church leaders." He writes, "While this type of informal dialogue perhaps has more potential in making a difference with regard to Christian life and witness in India, sadly very little attention is given to informing, equipping, and mobilizing Christians in India to undertake such informal dialogue with people of other faiths."[9]

I suggest that there are models that have worked elsewhere which incorporated an informal approach effectively in organized dialogues. One such model is the Interreligious dialogue in Tomsk, Siberia. Roman Bykov shows how over ten years, informal dialogue has brought about change for the better among 40 different religious groups that meet in Tomsk.[10] He writes, "formal dialogue, [which] is held regularly (several times a year) by the authorities in different countries, but is a kind of declarative and ineffective in building the harmonious relations between religious and ethnical groups."[11] He further notes, "A special role was played by scientists, who have created a neutral space where religious representatives are able to engage in equal dialogue and strive to

---

[7] Sen, "Gods, Gurus, Prophets and the Poor...," 2.
[8] Aghamkar, "Hindu-Christian Dialogue in India."
[9] *Ibid.*
[10] Roman Bykov, "Interreligious dialogue in Siberia: The experience of constructing an informal communication space" (April 20, 2020), accessed October 9, 2021, https://doc-research.org/2020/04/interreligious-dialogue-siberia-experience-constructing-informal-communication-space/.
[11] *Ibid.*

achieve a common understanding."[12] Describing the history and technology of creating interreligious dialogue, Bykov shows the positive effects of such activities or the social functions of informal dialogue.[13]

Another model is peace talks. For instance, Heini Lehtinen writes, "Today, most peace processes consist of various levels of dialogues, some of which link to official high-level talks, while others take place in parallel. Dialogues have become fairly localised as conflicts are being addressed where they often emerge – on the grassroots and community level."[14] Lehtinen draws upon Miriam Bensky's experience of having worked for the United Nations, the Centre for Humanitarian Dialogue, and in non-governmental organizations. Lehtinen notes that "Miriam Bensky has worked both on grassroots peacebuilding and international conflict resolution. In her career, she has focused on designing and facilitating various dialogues and diplomatic engagements, and supporting large-scale multilateral peace processes."[15] Bensky suggests that "There is often a mosaic of various different dialogue initiatives, which create or support conflict resolution both on the national and regional levels." She continues, "Even if the international news follow the big, official negotiations between, for example, the United States and the Taliban, there are usually many parallels, back-door and more informal side dialogues going on in the background." She concludes, "Probably most of the deals are made in those side conversations, not at the official roundtables in fancy conference rooms."[16] Lehtinen notes that informal dialogue formats involved choosing a location conducive to peace dialogues or spatial elements that contribute to a sense of respect, trust, or care; choosing building architecture that provides such informal spaces where feelings of security, confidentiality, and trust are built; using technology such as mobile platforms such as Signal, WhatsApp, Telegram or other more or less secure messaging apps., and; involving cross-disciplinary introductions and opportunities to network between professionals working in different sectors.[17]

I suggest that the above models might be helpful to study and apply in Christian witness. The church could learn from such informal communication methods to enrich its efforts in its Christian witness with people of its own or other faiths. Next, as already mentioned above, informal communication is vital in interactions with grassroots both in rural and urban contexts. On these, I would like to draw some thoughts and insights from my experience as well as others.

---

[12] *Ibid.*
[13] *Ibid.*
[14] Heini Lehtinen, "Changing spaces of peace dialogues – From formal to informal" (April 12, 2020), accessed October 9, 2021, https://medium.com/ravenandwood/changing-spaces-of-peace-dialogues-28f449ef8ac5.
[15] *Ibid.*
[16] Quoted in Lehtinen, "Changing spaces of peace dialogues – From formal to informal."
[17] Lehtinen, "Changing spaces of peace dialogues – From formal to informal."

Interreligious Dialogue and Rural Settings

In my article "Informal Dialogue in Rural India," I analysed reflexively my experience at Ramandoddi village in a Hindu rural setting.[18] Here, I revisit the same topic but reflect on my experience in a different place, Mugulapally, a village predominantly consisting of Hindus. I see my ministry from 1987-1995 in rural settings as both formal and informal interreligious interactions with the villagers. As Christian workers, individuals and groups visit villages, meeting known acquaintances and unknown people becomes inevitable. There are multiple layers to informal interactions in a rural setting that must be understood and used in our witness. We encounter the social structures and power relations in villages and are drawn into informal dialogue with them. First, I discuss ministry in the context of the institute in the middle of villages. Second, I discuss ministry in the context of villages.

The Context

Like most villages, the surrounding villages were multi-caste Hindu villages. There were a few single-caste villages. There were fewer villages with Muslims. Then Hindutva, a right-wing Hindu ideology was spreading to the remote villages, especially wherever Christian presence was felt.

The Ministry in Villages

Establishing a cross-culture training institute was part of the mission work I was involved in. This activity by the mission to establish the training institute informally communicated to the villagers that Christians and the church had come into their midst. The Outreach Training Institute (OTI) was also an opportunity to meet people's needs. It was a sort of listening to the non-verbal requests of the villagers. This rapport with people facilitated informal dialogue in the context of ministry in villages.

Informal Dialogue with the Villagers

A woman from the Mugulapally village invited us to share God's word with her family. Many people from this village worked on the building project of the OTI. One of the trainee teams headed by my wife and I prayed about it and went into the village for the first time.

Informal Dialogue with an Individual in the Village

An old woman was one of the first we met on the way to the village. She said she knew that we were from the church, for that was how the OTI was known to

---

[18] John Arun Kumar, "Informal Dialogue in Rural India," in *EAST MEETS EAST: In the Heartland of Hinduism Evangelical Interfaith Dialogue* 2:2 (2011), https://fullerstudio.fuller.edu/response-informal-dialogue-in-rural-india/.

the people in the area. Upon seeing us, she wanted us to visit her home and pray with her for her adult son, who had gone missing for more than a year. Here I see the chance meeting with an unknown person and entering into conversation as part of an informal dialogue in ministry. Meaning and meaningfulness of actions are important parts of informal dialogue in ministry.

Informal Dialogue between Groups

Unbeknown to us, at the time, there was a non-discursive informal dialogue taking place between two groups – the dissenting villagers and us as a team. The villagers had witnessed that we complied with the request for prayer by one of their own. Next, we moved into the house of one of their own who had invited us. At this point, the non-discursive informal dialogue turned into discursive informal dialogue as well. As I was sharing God's Word, there was an interruption by someone asking me to stop and come out of the house. This I did on the condition that they allow me to first finish sharing the Word. There was a young man, who had sent word for me to come out of the house, with a sickle ready to strike me as I complied with the request. Tension prevailed. Within the villager's house, they witnessed the women of the visiting team praying for my safety as I went out to face the angry young man, and for their own safety, and for the people gathered outside. The activity of praying was non-discursively playing its role in the informal dialogue. Typically, the young man said he was speaking for the whole village. However, he was representing the voices of some of the villagers who were opposed to the Christian presence in the village. The informal group dialogue was actually between the Hindutva ideology proponent and the Christians, me and us. The occasion in this informal group dialogue also clarified a mistaken identity: the villagers pointed out that I was a new visitor to the village and was not the Christian worker who visited them regularly. I appealed to the older people, who were onlookers, to check out the reasonableness of our visit to the village and our actions there. In the end, the young man and I both shook hands before our team left the village. Although we did not visit the village for a year after that incident, the villagers from that village who knew us kept us informed of the developments in the village. We learned from them that the woman's missing son had returned to her, and that the woman was pleased.

This experience taught me that villages have multiple informal nondiscursive and discursive intra-religious and inter-religious dialogues operative both at individual and group levels involving social and power structures. There is potential for conflicts and conflict resolution. Requests form an important part of the informal dialogue in ministry. Requests from the people included requests to visit them, pray for them, share from the Bible and help with their existential needs and problems, such as health, marriage, education and work. Requests did not always present themselves in the first encounter with people. Trust has to be built before this happens. I suggest that prayer is part of an informal dialogue. Christian workers must consider prayer as a form of informal religious dialogue in their ministerial praxis.

Interreligious Dialogue in the Grassroots

In multi-faith villages the informal dynamics between the various religious and caste communities are instructive. The OTI teams' visits to the surrounding villages included staying in villages for a couple of weeks at a stretch and weekends over the training course to have a first-hand experience of rural life and people. In my experience with the OTI team, I found that the villagers were generally quite comfortable with other religious groups around. There was a Muslim tomb of a local saint near the village where both Muslims and Hindus frequented and offered prayers because of its popularity for answering prayers. Here, a religious dialogue takes place because of the existential needs and belief in the efficacy of prayers without regard for religion. I also found that the villagers had high regard for Christian schools, hospitals and churches.

Muthuraj Swamy has shown how current categories of formal interreligious dialogue ignore and do not take into account the grassroots realities that are relational, multicultural, multi-religious and with multiple identities. Swamy writes that interreligious relationships among people in a *Gramam* (village) are spontaneous, "They do not need any agency or a 'common platform' to relate with their neighbours from other religions, nor is prior knowledge of religions expected. Multiplicity is just part of everyday life."[19] He argues that there are lessons that grassroots could teach about dialogue and resources for conflict resolution that are generally ignored in formal interreligious dialogue efforts.[20] He writes, "In opposition to the claim by dialogue proponents that the grassroots people need an awareness of dialogue to enable relatedness," Swamy observes that the people of a *Gramam* already relate well with one another.[21] He suggests that "Without knowing what dialogue is, and without being influenced by elite forms of dialogue, the people at the grassroots exhibit knowledge of their religious neighbours, learn from each other, contribute to each other and live in solidarity."[22] From this, he notes that "the issues of syncretism and relativism do not affect them – but this does not mean that they do not have any faith traditions. Rather it indicates that people at the grassroots do not primarily understand their identity and their neighbours' identity in terms of exclusivist religion."[23] I would add that the villagers' identity primarily lies in shared humanity and human needs and informal communication is part and parcel of it.

Interreligious Dialogue and Urban Settings

I note here from my personal experiences reflectively. Informal conversations and observations are avenues to understanding the worldviews of the other. This is very important in a multi-religious and multicultural context. Recently, a Hindu house owner's family had to ask one of the tenants, a Christian worker, to

---

[19] Muthuraj Swamy, "Religion, Religious Conflicts and Interreligious Dialogue in India: An Interrogation" (PhD diss., University of Edinburgh, April 2012), 245-246.
[20] *Ibid.* 31.
[21] *Ibid.* 252.
[22] *Ibid.*
[23] *Ibid.*

leave. The tenant had a woman visiting him regularly who was not his wife. The owner and his wife said they regard God and Jesus, but behaviour such as their tenant's was unacceptable. From this informal talk, I observe that Hindus distinguish between God and God's servant. They recognize God's holiness and human weaknesses. The landlady said she loves to listen to Christian songs. She had visited Roman Catholic churches to offer prayers. She has a relative who was a Christian. In this, there seems to be openness to accepting Jesus Christ as a god, offering prayers, visiting churches and enjoying Christian music. This shows that not all Hindus have bought into the ideas of *Hindutva*. There are Hindus who have a secular outlook, which is the way a large proportion of the Hindu majority in India are. Here, they were not only sharing their concerns but also explaining their action to my wife and I because we are Christians. It showed us their regard for Christian workers and Christians but disapproved of their improper social behaviour. The informal talk (dialogue) could be categorized here as discursive in nature.

Nondiscursive observations are also important in understanding the other in interreligious interactions. In this, the observation of symbols and actions used by the other becomes important to understanding the other. For example, the house owner lady visited us with a couple of women, her relatives from her extended family. The first thing one of the older of them observed was a lack of any images of deities in our living room and that led to a mini discussion amongst themselves about whether we worship God. Then they went on to ask us whether we worship the images of Jesus. Another instance involves a shop owner in my area with a picture frame displayed prominently on one of his shelves. It has pictures of a Sacred Heart Jesus (commonly used in Roman Catholic homes), Ganesh (the Hindu deity with an elephant head), and the Kaaba stone of the holy shrine of Haj. I observed that the shop owner was not offering *puja* (which he offers daily to his Hindu deities placed on a separate shelf) to the picture frame of Jesus and the Kaaba stone.[24] On asking about this, the shop owner said he did not want to offend the God of Christianity and Islam by offering puja to those images. Similarly, during my doctoral research, I saw that some of the Hindu homes in Kothanur had framed pictures of Jesus kept along with other images of Hinduism. But care is taken not to apply any *bindi* mark to the picture of Jesus. On inquiring about the reason for their practice, my interviewees gave the same reply as the shop owner. Then there were others who made no such distinction and offered *puja* to Jesus along with all their deities.

An Indian secular view is evident in the above examples. Those who hold this view have made room or accommodated images of Christ in their sacred space as a silent expression of their understanding, or shall we say, faith. These informal observations and discussions led us to understand each other better and provided opportunities to give reasons for our faith. However, there are also those who have moved on from such a viewpoint to embrace following Jesus Christ only, as we can see in the instance given here below.

---

[24] The Sanskrit word *puja* refers to the worship ritual performed by Hindus to offer devotion and prayer to a deity.

My wife and I hired an *autorickshaw* (a motorised three-wheeled public conveyance) and found that in the inside front of the vehicle was Jesus' picture and a bible verse. Furthermore, there were enough clues to indicate that it belonged to a Christian. We then asked the driver if he was a Christian. He answered in the affirmative and went on to say that all his family members were from a Hindu background but were now followers of Christ. His sister was the first in their family to follow the Lord thirteen years ago. His brother-in-law, a Brahmin by caste, was also a follower of Jesus. He said he did not have to go seeking God, but God came seeking him and answered his prayers. Since then, they have been followers of Jesus. When paying his fare, he did not want more money than what was due to him when we offered him a little extra. This example shows how it was not blind faith or any fraudulent conversion but a genuine seeking of the truth that led his family to follow Jesus. While some Hindus see being secular as part of being Hindu and hold a pluralistic view equating Jesus and other gods as being on par, this young man and his family chose to embrace Jesus Christ alone as their God and Saviour.

From my study of some of the testimonies of Christians from Hindu backgrounds, I gather that one of the ways they have become followers of Jesus is through informal friendships and family relationships. In one such instance, my Hindu friend Sunder, his mother and his sister became serious followers of Jesus after they started reading the Bible. Following this, they faced heavy opposition from his father, risking their lives for their faith in Jesus. All that they needed was access to the Bible. Once they were introduced to the Bible, they began reading it themselves and made an informed decision to become Christians.

My research findings on the lives of Christians and their faith in the workplace show that informal interactions with superiors, peers and subordinates were opportunities to share their faith with others.[25] Sreekumaran Nair, a former Rashtriya Swayam Sevak (RSS), a right-wing Hindu organization worker, suggests that informal contacts and interactions are fruitful in doing missions, even among RSS workers. He writes that there are many well-educated, disciplined and keen-minded individuals among RSS cadres. Some of them are open to welcoming the gospel if they are approached and presented with the gospel informally.[26] These encounters reveal how God is at work at the local informal level when at state, national, and international levels, Hindutva ideas seem to take centre stage in politics and world affairs. However, it also suggests that it might be the case that God is at work at informal levels among employees, businessmen and women, diplomats and other ideologues at the state, national and international levels.

---

[25] John Arun Kumar, "Hindu-Christian Relationships at the Workplace." A paper presented at the Global Workplace Forum, Lausanne Movement, Manila, 2020.
[26] Nair, Shreekumaran, "A Study on Hindutva Ideology and Practices with Special Reference to Rashtriya Swayamsevak Sangh: A Missiological Assessment, 1980 to 2007" (Master of Theology diss, South Asia Institute of Advanced Christian Studies, 2009).

Jesus is our Model for Informal Dialogue

My definition of mission, drawn from the great commission, is that the disciples of Jesus are sent to all nations to teach them what Jesus has taught, baptizing them in the name of the Father, Son, and Holy Spirit. Here baptism is to be understood as immersing the nations in the teachings of the Lord Jesus Christ on the Father, the Son and the Holy Spirit. The imagery here is drawn from flooding rice crops needing water 24/7 (Graham Hulse chapel talk, SAIACS, 2020). I suggest this could mean a constant engagement with people, teaching them what the Lord Jesus taught. The engagement could take varied forms. Jesus used various methods, which included both formal and informal dialogues. The Christian church could do best by following him.

Many of Jesus' actions were performed informally. He went to people in their settings and living spaces and participated in their life activities and celebrations. He did not use set and elaborate ritual patterns or practices but used simple activities of prayer in all his interactions with God and human beings. He invited people into his living space. He practiced his spiritual habits of prayer and fasting (the Bible informs us that he often went away from his disciples and prayed alone in the early hours). He read from the scriptures. He listened to the requests of people and offered help, healing and deliverance. Jesus engaged with people in both discursive and nondiscursive forms.

A Proposal for Informal Dialogue

Below are some suggestions for informal dialogue drawn from insights from the literature and experiences mentioned in this paper.

Suppose we are thinking in terms of organized interreligious meetings, the model in the interreligious dialogue in Tomsk, Siberia, seems to be a fruitful one to attempt this in an organized way.[27] Bykov's suggestion, when applied to our context, might bring about change among different religious groups at local, national and international levels. Those working on peace talks can draw insights from the model discussed by Lehtinen based on Bensky's experience. Official high-level talks, parallel talks, grassroots talks and community-level talks are opportunities to facilitate informal dialogues by providing informal spaces, ambiance and time.[28]

Rural settings offer umpteen opportunities for informal dialogue and interactions. The basic form of interaction is informal, so this has to be lived out with those living in such contexts. Openness and readiness to engage with people, both individuals and groups, in conversations are very important. Listening to them and if there is a request that is doable and right to do, being able to do it will help. Entertaining visitors at homes, institutions, worship places and our living areas, such as our villages, offers opportunities for others to see things done differently and learn from that experience without using words. Dialogues in rural settings, perhaps in other settings as well, must incorporate inter-community rather than interreligious language; the need to recognize and

---

[27] Bykov, "Interreligious dialogue in Siberia."
[28] Lehtinen, "Changing spaces of peace dialogues – From formal to informal."

deal with conflicts as real-life rather than religious conflicts; and the need to recognize and utilize real-life experiences of people.

On the whole Christian witness in the context of India will be enriched and able to make fresh attempts by incorporating informal dialogue methods. It is a biblical pattern exemplified by Jesus and the apostles. We will do well to follow the Master in this.

Church and Social Justice: Consensus with the Holy Spirit

E.D. Solomon

This contribution presents a real-life example of interreligious engagement in India. It discusses church and social justice with reflections from a public square incident involving a contention over the burial rite of a certain Papi Reddy at Ahamrai village in 1999. Here, social justice and tradition conflicted. The tension arose over whether to respect the deceased's last wish for a Christian burial or to execute a high caste burial as pressed by the Patel caste elders. My narrative below will clarify the stakeholders in the episode.

Secondly, social justice is viewed here from an Anabaptist seminary's engagement in society. Here, "consensus" and "solidarity" are used interchangeably. It reflects on how a theological seminary provides "solidarity" to the bereaved Papi Reddy family. The action of the seminarians represents the national church's witness. Reddy's immediate family's desire was to respect the dead person's last wish lest they hurt his eternity. Consensus with the Holy Spirit is interpreted as our "advocacy" in favour of the bereaved family (Jn 14:16; 1 Jn 2:1). This was in contrast to the Patel caste elders' counterclaim to perform burial their caste way. Several rounds of negotiations ensued. In engaging dialogue patterns, I will employ Paulo Freire's terms, "biophily" to mean "affirmation of life" and "necrophily" to mean "killing of life," found in his influential work, *Pedagogy of the Oppressed* (1993). By biophily, we mean affirming the family's desire to bury the dead in a Christian way. Necrophily is taken as a counterargument of the larger caste group against a forty-member seminary team standing with the bereaved.

Thirdly, this paper does not deal with judgments delivered at law courts, where judges interpret the law in favour or against someone or in the interest of public litigation. The law ensures liberty, equality and fraternity to all citizens. Supreme Court Justice (Retired) Kurian Joseph vouches for two aspects of the law. The first aspect is to go by the written codes like the Pharisees were practicing during Jesus' time (Mk 12:18-27). The second aspect is to follow the spirit of the Indian Constitution. Justice Kurian summarized "the spirit of the law" as "compassion."[1]

Fourthly, by "church", I mean both *mater fidelium* ("an institution") and *mater coetus* ("an organism"), as theologian Luis Berkhof suggests.[2] However,

---

[1] Kurian Joseph, "The Idea of Justice in the Constitution of India: A Christian Perspective", Zoom lecture on 12 March 2022. Joseph went on to point to Jesus as the best interpreter of the spirit of the Jewish law as compassion. He claimed his insights come from his Roman Catholic roots in Kerala. Joseph served in the Supreme Court of India during 2013-2018.

[2] Calvin P. Van Reken "The Church's Role in Social Justice," in *Calvin Theological Journal* 34 (1999), 198-202. Reken uses "church work" to mean a task assigned to an

in this paper, I will focus on the organic function of a church, represented by the seminary group, in resolving the village conflict over the type of funeral to perform. A church, for me, is basically "a communion of saints" in Jesus Christ. However, it would benefit our understanding to peel what an *ekklesia* means,

> The Greek word ekklēsia, which came to mean church, was originally applied in the Classical period to an official assembly of citizens. In the Septuagint (Greek) translation of the Old Testament (3rd-2nd century BCE), the term ekklēsia is used for the general assembly of the Jewish people, especially when gathered for a religious purpose such as hearing the law (e.g., Deuteronomy 9:10, 18:16). In the New Testament it is used of the entire body of believing Christians throughout the world (e.g., Matthew 16:18), of the believers in a particular area (e.g., Acts 5:11), and also of the congregation meeting in a particular house – the "house-church" (e.g., Romans 16:5).[3]

An *ekklesia,* as per this quote, indicates (i) a secular assembly of a town, (ii) a religious assembly of Jews to hear the law, (iii) a community of believers in Christ in a village or world and (iv) a gathering of a house-church. But how is justice processed through consensus in a village church? In the following section, I will clarify my thoughts on social justice, consensus and panchayat.

Social Justice, Consensus and Panchayat

In this section, I will draw insights from my previous work, *Change and Continuity* (2012). One of my primary concerns in that volume was interpreting how a church *panchayat* resolves a dispute.[4] In answering this question, I intersect my empirical data with that of my mentor late Paul G. Hiebert (1932-2007). Hiebert finds "structure and integration" in Konduru[5] village of Andhra Pradesh. He found that traditional *panchayats* process litigation via consensus. Here "consensus" refers to a "group solidarity in sentiment and belief."[6] Consensus is a community hermeneutic.

By "social justice," I mean standing with the sufferers. W. Schneider rightly takes the Greek word *krima* (Κριμα) and especially its indicative *krino* (κρινω), referring to the LXX translation of three Hebrew terms, namely, *sapat, din* and *rib.* These terms concern themselves with "resolving a dispute" and "standing

---

employee by the church. He also uses "kingdom work" to mean the job assigned to believers by God. Reken understands the primary call of the church to bear witness to the Gospel. But a local church shall not speak for the synod or the national Reformed church. The synod may either "condemn" or "commend" on certain policies of a government.

[3] "Church-Christianity", accessed January 22, 2023, https://www.britannica.com/topic/church-Christianity.

[4] Etala David Solomon, *Change and Continuity: Influences on Self-Identity of Christian Dalits of Madiripuram Village in South India, 1950-2005* (Delhi: ISPCK, 2012), 165-194.

[5] Paul G. Hiebert, *Konduru: Structure and integration in a South Indian village* (Minneapolis: University of Minnesota Press, 1974), 101-130.

[6] "Consensus", accessed March 18, 2022, https://www.britannica.com/topic/church-Christianity.

with the oppressed." The real intention of *krima*, then, is to attempt to "restore peace in a community." Schneider elaborates further by saying,

> Thus krino, to judge, acquired a meaning which went beyond its general Gk. usage, for din means not only to judge, but also to punish, wrangle, vindicate, and obtain justice for a person (Gen. 15:14; 2 Sam. 19:9; Gen. 30:6; Deut. 32:36; Ps. 54:3; Jer. 5:28). Rib means to quarrel, to litigate, to carry on a lawsuit (Gen. 26:21; Jdg. 8:1;21:22; 1 Sam. 24:16). Sapat, which occurs the most frequently, adds still further shades of meaning, so that to judge comes to mean "to rule" (Exod. 2:14; 1 Sam. 8:20; 2 Sam. 15:4,6). He who judges brings salvation, peace and deliverance, especially to the persecuted and oppressed (cf. Deut. 10:18).[7]

Second, Schneider understands *krima* as functional justice for Israel. He sees "restoring peace" as its primary function. However, in difficult cases, it does mean banishing an arrogant member. He writes,

> In Israel all justice was originally dispensed not according to absolute moral standards but with a view to restoring peace within the community concerned, whether the family, the tribe, or the nation. In difficult cases it meant removing the offending member. After the conquest justice was dispensed partly in the context of family and tribe by the heads of families and tribal elders, and partly in the context of the local community by the elders sitting in the gate of a town or village, all full citizens having right to speak (Ruth 4:1ff).[8]

Third, Schneider locates God's character as the source of justice. YHWH's mercy motivates him to ensure the safety and security of his chosen people, especially on "the *day* of the Lord" (*hemera*). Further, Schneider views God as the judge and sovereign over all humanity (*ethne*),

> In Israel all justice is ascribed to God: Yahweh is Lord and judge (Deut. 1:17). As judge he helps his people (Jdg. 11:27; 2 Sam. 18:31). He never deviates from justice (Ps. 7:12) and will not suffer his honour to be brought into disrepute. Heaven and earth or the peoples of the earth are often called upon to act as a tribunal (Isa. 1:2; Jer. 2:12; Mic. 6:1; Ps. 50:1-6). He judges the nations (Gen. 11:1 ff; Ps. 67:5; Amos 1:2; Joel 4:2; Mal. 3.2 ff), especially on the "day of Yahweh", when he will destroy all ungodliness (Isa. 2:12-18; 13:9; Jer. 46:10 Ezek. 30:3ff; Zeph. 1:7-18; Present, art. hemera). He comes to the aid of anyone suffering violence and injustice (Gen. 4:9ff). One must submit to his inscrutable judgment (Job). His judgments are just, i.e., they are in harmony with his faithfulness, whereby he espouses the cause of his chosen people, guides them and ensures their safety. Thus, God's judgment is motivated by love, grace and mercy, and its outcome is salvation (Isa. 30:18; Ps. 25:6-9; 33:5;103:6ff; 146:7). "He will vindicate his people and have compassion on his servants" (Deut. 32:36 RSV).[9]

Fourth, going ahead, I am concerned with how *aletheian* (ἀλήθειαν; practice truth) is linked to justice-making. It is not surprising then that the *Practical Word Studies in the New Testament* uses *aletheian* to refer to "truthfulness" in society, which means the "practical application" of truthfulness in a community living,

---

[7] W. Schneider, "Judgement," in *The International Dictionary of New Testament Theology*, Vol.2 (G-Pre), Gen. ed. Colin Brown (Grand Rapids, MI: Regency,1986), 363.
[8] *Ibid*, 363.
[9] *Ibid*, 363-364.

The judgment of God – of the only living and true God – is according to truth. God's judgment will be executed in perfect justice. The word "justice" (aletheian) means true as opposed to false. It means what really is; what actually exists; what exactly takes place. God's judgment is perfectly just, exactly what it should be, nothing more and nothing less. His judgment is based upon...
- What really happens
- What the facts are
- What actually takes place
- What a person really is within his heart
- What the person actually did.[10]

Another term that concerns us is "panchayat". It refers to a traditional village council consisting of five wise elders. It is the legal court of a village. There are two types of *panchayats*: traditional and modern. Since independence (1947), India has come to experience the second type, *naya* (modern) panchayat. A major difference between traditional and *naya* panchayat is the years of service. In a traditional *panchayat*, elders are chosen for a year while the *naya panchayat* selects their leaders for five years. *Naya panchayat* is based on democratic principles. The majority vote decides the winner or loser. Moreover, votes can be manipulated by the rich and influential, implying that justice can also be played around with. The traditional *panchayat* has been functional for thousands of years in village India. Hiebert notes that for village India, kings and kingdoms rise and fall, but the *panchayat* way of leadership keeps the village going.[11] Here, a charismatic leader, the *sarpanch*, usually heads the *panchayat*. Traditionally, he is an elderly person, of a high caste, who, over the years, has earned respect through impartial judgments.[12] The traditional *panchayat* legal decrees are based on consensus. In a court of justice, the "winner-loser" is the locomotive, while the traditional *panchayat* focuses on justice *and* social harmony in a village. In this paper, I am concerned with the traditional *panchayat*.

Consensus Ensures Social Cohesion

A *panchayat* functions on "social cohesion" as its core principle. Protagonists and adversaries need to understand this reality. A course of action will have the support of all or major parties involved. So, a variance of opinion is possible. If a *panchayat* fails to arrive at a consensus, its decisions are ineffectual. Its power ultimately lies effectively in social ostracism, not in fines or punishments.[13] When disputes are amicably settled, the *panchayat* elders, proponents and litigants celebrate the resolution with a traditional drink, *kallu* (the sap of a palm tree). This drink is usually purchased with part of the money levied as a fine on the guilty person or party. By participating in the cultural drink, harmony is restored in the village.

---

[10] Leadership Ministries Worldwide, *Practical Word Studies in the New Testament: The Outline Bible Five Translation,* Vol. 1 (A-K) (Chattanooga, TN: Leadership Ministries Worldwide, 1998), 1177.
[11] Solomon, *Change and Continuity*, 165.
[12] Hiebert, *Konduru*, 103.
[13] *Ibid.* 103.

Additionally, I have found five types of legal systems in my research village. Listing them would be helpful: (i) *Kula* (caste) *panchayat*, (ii) *Kisan panchayat*, (iii) *Gram panchayat*, (iv) Church *panchayat* and (v) Reddy-Christian Dalit *panchayat*. I locate my discussion to type (i) above: the *Kula panchayat* at Ahamrai village. It was a traditional honour-shame debate within the Patel caste.

Ahamrai Village Narrative

Papi Reddy died on February 3, 1999. He was a believer in Jesus Christ but died before his baptism. He and his wife Sara, their son, Bhimsen and their daughter-in-law, Jayasheeli, had been led to faith in Jesus Christ by a Christian medical doctor. Papi Reddy belonged to the Patel caste. Traditionally this caste was responsible for law and order in the village. Before breathing his last, he requested a Christian funeral. Respecting his last wish, the family asked their spiritual father, the doctor, to arrange for a Christian rite, who, in turn, requested the local Anabaptist seminary for moral support and to officiate the funeral ceremony.

By midday, Papi Reddy's warrior caste relatives, about a hundred and fifty, kept pouring in to pay their last respects. The relatives pressed for a caste burial. However, this was contrary to the last wish of the deceased and his bereaving family members. Patel clan elders, represented by the *Talari Reddy* duo,[14] were vehemently against a Christian funeral and asserted that the family would not be allowed to dig a grave for burial in their ancestral cemetery if they did not agree to their demand. Since the family was unwilling, the duo even objected to the coffin being lifted to be carried it to the burial site until late evening.

Meanwhile, the delegation of seminary students, of which I was one, arrived in batches, before finally numbering forty. Shalem, a senior faculty led the team of students. The village was a few kilometres away from the seminary. Upon arriving, we learned that the caste elders were pressing for a caste burial. That being the scenario, the seminary team entered Papi Reddy's huge traditional house for a dialogue with the caste leaders. A critical realist, Shalem, the seminary faculty, advised the bereaving family that it was okay to listen to their clan members' advice for a caste burial and that Jesus would understand their predicament. But the bereaving family was displeased with the counsel, lest they hurt the honour of their dead who wanted a Christian rite.

Several rounds of dialogue ensued without a solution. The day was drawing to an end with sunset at about six in the evening. Not finding a breakthrough, the *Talari Reddy* duo cautioned the seminarians,

> It is because of your presence the family is unyielding for a Patel caste funeral. Moreover, Papi Reddy was not baptized. So, a Christian funeral is out of the question. You would do well also to recall the horrible treatment meted out to the

---

[14] *Talari* is the head of a clan, or a party. There were two who spoke for hundred and fifty Patel caste group.

late Graham Staines and two of his young sons on the night of January 23, 1999. And you better dismiss yourselves from the scene.[15]

In response, the seminary leader replied,

We have no issues with your claim for a caste funeral. But let the family agree to it. In the event of the family agreeing to a Hindu funeral, we will not object but stand in solidarity with the bereaved family. We will walk behind your funeral procession. We will pay homage after your ceremony is over.[16]

With that understanding, the seminary team moved out of the house for some time. However, the family was relentless in their Christian faith. So, the caste leaders threatened the new believers with a "social boycott." Furthermore, it was becoming very dark, and in villages, no honourable funeral would take place in darkness. But the novice disciples were not bothered about the night. Finally, giving up hope, the leaders of the Patel caste informed the seminary leader,

Perform the funeral your way. We refuse to participate. But bury the body of Papi Reddy not in our ancestral cemetery but at *Ura bondala gadda* where the low castes or back-sliders or immigrants are buried.[17]

This act amounted to desecrating the last respects of a dead. Surprisingly, the bereaved family felt relieved, not minding caste displeasure. For us, the seminarians, it was a litmus test of whether to betray the bereaved family or risk violence. We chose solidarity with the bereaved and the forty students supported the family's decision. Shalem had to act quickly and ask us to dig the grave. Adding to our challenge, the "common" cemetery was a kilometre away from the family's house. However, we had the tomb ready by 8 pm. The funeral was performed amidst fears of a communal riot. But it went peacefully. Following the burial, the women folk asked the Shalem, the seminary teacher to break the *bangles* of the widow and help her take off the *mangal sutra* to symbolize Sara's widowhood.

Reminiscing on the event, we feel honoured to have stood in solidarity with the bereaved family. As a result, the family continues to be a strong witness to Christ. However, the interest here is to missiologically discern what was going on in our witness.

Freire's Biophilic and Necrophilic Pedagogy

Firstly, the above episode presents us with some leads in *ekklesial* engagement in conflict resolution. It showed that no conflict resolution is risk-free. It could

---

[15] On the night of January 23, 1999, Graham Staines and his two sons were burnt alive Manoharpur village, Keonjhar district in Orissa (present day Odisha). See the report of the incident in *India Today*, "Staines' Killing: Murder of Australian missionary and his two sons in Orissa shocks India", accessed February 4, 2022, https://www.indiatoday.in/magazine/cover-story/story/19990208-staines-killing-murder-of-australian-missionary-and-his-two-sons-in-orissa-shocks-india-780092-1999-02-08 (Papi Reddy died within a fortnight of Staines' death. So, the commotion was violent and risky).

[16] Thus, Shalem, the seminary faculty tried to pacify the commotion. But to no result.

[17] This was the version of the clan leaders who were the closest relatives of Papi Reddy.

result in additional pain for the oppressed/bereaved. In this case, the bereaved family was disowned by the Patel clan. Thankfully, the *gram panchayat* did not ostracize them, but distances were kept. Secondly, the episode shows that the Gospel divides people on account of Christ. We experienced what Freire calls biophilic and necrophilic dialogue. Thirdly, the event presented the seminary students with onsite teaching, something like what Jesus would do with his twelve disciples. Freire also advocates the necessity of engagement not only in the classroom but also with our native cultures.[18] My passion here is to connect Freire's perceptions with the church and social justice because a true pedagogy is context specific.

Freire's biophilic dialogue implies the church's necessity to discern social justice through critical dialogue. He distinguishes necrophilic conversations as antiphonal to biophilic dialogue. Let me begin with his distaste for necrophilic pedagogy. First, necrophily begins with an inhuman premise. A necrophilic education is contra development. Freire says that a "banking type of education" treats men and women as mere objects. The referent here is to the Patel clan refusing to hear the bereaved family's Christian witness. The family came to know the Lord through an experience whereby one of Bhimsen's sons was healed of a chronic disease. Necrophily kills life. It is against what Erich Fromm calls "biophily". Freire states,

> characterized by growth in a structured, functional manner, the necrophilous person loves all that does not grow, all that is mechanical. The necrophilous person is driven by the desire to transform the organic into inorganic, to approach life mechanically, as if all living persons were things ... Memory, rather than experience; having, rather than being, is what counts. The necrophilous person can relate to an object – a flower or a person – only if he possesses it; hence a threat to his possession is a threat to himself; if he loses possession, he loses contact with the world ... He loves control, and in the act of controlling he kills life.[19]

Second, Freire critiques necrophilous education as negative.[20] Such education is digressive. It reproduces imitation and kills the imagination. Thirdly, there is neither life nor variety in necrophily. It kills the self-affirmation of a human.

---

[18] Freire, Paulo. *Pedagogy of the Oppressed*, trans. Myra Bergman Ramos (New Delhi: Thomson Press India Ltd, 1993). Freire's pedagogy is a teaching method for social revolution.
[19] *Ibid.* 50.
[20] *Ibid.* 46. The necrophilic education method is explained in ten negative characters. It mirrors an oppressive society where (i) the teacher teaches and the students are taught; (ii) the teacher knows everything and the students know nothing; (iii) the teacher thinks and the students are thought about; (iv) the teacher talks and the students listen meekly; (v) the teacher disciplines and the students are disciplined; (vi) the teacher chooses and enforces his choice, and the students comply; (vii) the teacher acts and the students have the illusion of acting through the action of the teacher; (viii) the teacher chooses the program content, and the students (who were not consulted) adapt it; (ix) the teacher confuses the authority of knowledge with his or her own professional authority, which she or he sets in opposition to the freedom of the students; and (x) the teacher is the subject of the learning process, while the pupils are mere objects.

Fourthly, the world around a necrophilic is disconnected. In such contexts, Freire recommends *conscientazacao*.

Freire's *Conscientazacao*

Freire rightly says that everyone in praxis not only reflects on their "situationality" but "acts" on it.[21] We should understand Freire in his social context. For him, there are three dialogue partners.[22] Firstly, "sectarian rightists", who are fond of communal interests. Secondly, the "radical leftists", who categorize society into rich and poor or fascist and socialist groups. But neither the rightist nor the leftist dialogues would be successful if they did not conscientize their third dialogue partner, "the common citizen." This is where Freire introduces *conscientazacao* (critical conscientization) as transcending the (1) religious fanatic and (2) extremist communists.[23]

The third option is what Freire advocates. For him, any revolution must touch base with the lifeline of an average labourer/person. Moreover, change is "never a constant" but "in the making" through dialogue. Such critical dialogue would ensure true humanization. In the process of humanization, Freire proposes the value of *consceintizacao* because "[t]he awakening of critical consciousness leads the way to the expression of social discontents precisely because these discontents are real components of an oppressive situation."[24] In such a journey, Freire warrants true educationists to confront the culture of domination. Of course, he wants this engagement to be a cooperative effort with other transformers in dialogue.

Biophily Challenges the Culture of Domination

In light of the Patel caste hegemony, I agree with Freire's two-stage pedagogy. The first stage is for the oppressed to "unveil the world of oppression" but commit themselves to praxis toward transformation.[25] Praxis for Freire is both "reflection and action" in dialogue. In the second stage, Freire advises revolutionaries to "expulse the myths" created by the oppressor.[26] In this journey, he likes to unveil the consciousness of both the oppressor and the oppressed; thus, he states, "It must take into account their behaviour, their view of the world, and their ethics. A particular problem is the duality of the oppressed; they are contradictory, divided beings, shaped by and existing in a concrete situation of oppression and violence."[27] I concur with Freire when he says dialogue is an

---

[21] *Ibid.* 82.
[22] All three partners live in their separate "situations." Every group of people is situation produced. But interactions between them are necessary for change.
[23] Freire, *Pedagogy of the Oppressed*, pp. 35-39.
[24] *Ibid.* 10.
[25] *Ibid.* 41.
[26] *Ibid.* 28-29.
[27] *Ibid.* 29. Freire defines oppression as "Any situation in which 'A' objectively exploits 'B' or hinders his and her pursuit of self-affirmation. Such a situation in itself constitutes violence, even when sweetened by false generosity, because it interferes with

existential necessity, a method to transform a crisis. However, there are a few caveats that need to be considered. First, Freire's *pedagogy* is Latin American and not Asian. Though he identifies with the oppressed, his was a class and not a caste hegemony, as in the case of the incident at Ahamrai village. Second, Freire's *Pedagogy* is not concerned with the witness of the Indian church/seminary specifically. Thus, we would not be justified if we bind Freire to our ecclesial engagements. He aims to reform Brazilian society. His dream is more nationalistic than ours. Of course, I did sense in "caste funeral" reference to the fanatic Hindu nationalism in the *Talari* duo's discourse. For example, the duo invoked the cruel treatment meted out to Graham Staines. On the other hand, the seminary team leader offered the embrace of all humans in the Gospel. Third, unlike mine, Freire is not reflecting on an "on-the-spot" engagement in a South Indian village. He wrote *Pedagogy of the Oppressed* during his six-year political imprisonment. However, both of us are aligned in pedagogy and its goal. At the Ahamrai village funeral, our opponents and we exchanged differing worldviews. Nevertheless, my primary concern is to discern church and social justice as a consensus exercise with the work of the Holy Spirit.

Consensus is ancient wisdom for both Indians and Jews. It is vital in rural jurisprudence. According to Merriam-Webster, consensus means "a general agreement about something, an idea or opinion that is shared by all the people in a group."[28] It ensures implementation of the decision arrived at a village assembly. Unlike the law court decrees, *panchayat* rulings are better understood by the litigants. Hiebert concurs with M.N. Srinivas, who states that it is not that the "justice administered by the elders is always or even usually more just than the justice administered by the judges in urban law courts, but only that it is better understood by the litigants."[29]

Application of the Ahamrai Village Narrative

Firstly, consensus calls our attention to engagement in society beyond Christian charity. In the Papi Reddy case, it means engagement beyond the seminary classroom. It opens our eyes to look beyond the mission compound worldview, in which we have to prepare ourselves to converse beyond our comfort zones. It makes us open to engagement with people of other faiths and to advocate the values of the kingdom in the public square. Secondly, consensus calls for our solidarity with the oppressed, the sick and the bereaved family units against fanatic hermeneutics of the rightists or the leftists. Thirdly, our engagement calls for resistance to cultural hegemony. Fourthly, consensus becomes one of our praxis models. Our conversation partners are not just the evangelicals, the liberals or even the heretics but non-Christian friends, people with whom we share different faiths and ideologies and cultural values, and even at times,

---

the individual's ontological and historical vocation to be more fully human. With the establishment of a relationship of oppression, violence has *already* begun."

[28] "Consensus", accessed January 23, 2023, https://www.merriam-webster.com/dictionary/consensus.

[29] Hiebert, *Konduru,* 130.

mindsets. But as I see it, such a solidarity paradigm raises a critical question for us. How can we be sure of solidarity with the Holy Spirit's work in social justice?

Social Justice and the Holy Spirit

How would we align ecclesial decrees with the Holy Spirit's work? Let us explore mission principles from Acts 15:1-16:5. The following discussion is my re-reading of the work of the Holy Spirit within and above the ecclesial structure at Jerusalem.

Processing ecclesial jurisprudence through the work of the Holy Spirit is a true yardstick. In Christianity, we do see decision-making by consensus in the first Jerusalem Council (AD 49). How did the Council discern the unity of the global church and the integrity of the Gospel (Acts 15:22-31)? After a lengthy discussion, James, the half-brother of the Lord Jesus Christ and the moderator of the Council, ruled, "For it seemed good to the Holy Spirit and to us to lay on you no greater burden than these requirements…" (Acts 15:28). To me, James was saying, it is not enough for us to work in solidarity with human entities but in solidarity and obedience to the Holy Spirit. Thus, theologically, the Jerusalem decree was drafted in solidarity with the guidance of the Holy Spirit. Craig Keener observes that consensus was a common practice in the early church,

> The apostles don't rule without the elders, and both engage in vigorous debate, as Jewish teachers did in their schools. Jewish assemblies often sought to function by majority opinion or consensus among themselves rather than fiat. In later rabbinic schools, rabbis often had to agree to disagree, though submitting to majority opinion; this assembly seeks to achieve consensus (Acts 15:22).[30]

The consensus at the Jerusalem Council arrived after a *vehement* disagreement and long discussion (Acts 15:2, 7). What does that mean for the church and social justice today? I see a three-fold process.

Firstly, the Jerusalem Council *heard* the concern of the Judaizers over a long discussion (Acts 15:7a). They heard both the proponents' and opponents' views. The question at stake was whether or not "the gospel is imprisoned to the Jewish culture."[31] At the Syrian Antioch church, a few legalistic messianic Jews purporting to be from Jerusalem, demanded the proselytization of the gentile believers. Secondly, the process had to appraise the *witness* of the apostles (Acts 15:7b). Peter, Barnabas and Paul testified to miraculous signs and wonders wrought by them among the Gentiles even before their circumcision (Acts 15:12). Peter witnessed "the Holy Spirit fell even upon the Gentile hearers at Cornelius' house" (Acts 10:44 cf.15:8). Peter's testimony was,

- God *knows* every human *heart* (Acts 15:8a cf. 1 Sam. 15:7).

---

[30] Craig S. Keener, *The IVP Bible Background Commentary: New Testament*, second edition (Downers Grove, IL: IVP Academic, 2014), 365.
[31] See my take in "Contextualizing Ecclesiology: The Jerusalem Council, AD-49 (Acts 15:1-16:5)," in *The Yobel Spring: Festschrift to Rev. Dr. Chilkuri Vasantha Rao on his 50th Birthday*, Vol.2, eds P.S. Praveen, Royce M. Victor and Naveen Rao et al. (Hyderabad: ACTC/ISPCK, 2014), 467- 473.

- He *cleanses*[32] hearts through faith (Acts 15:9b).
- He *accepts* sinners on the basis of the "undeserved grace of the Lord Jesus Christ" (Acts 15:11b).
- He *does not discriminate* the uncircumcised from the circumcised. He empowers them with the Holy Spirit (Acts 15:8b).

Here Peter warned the Judaizers to "dare not challenge" the Holy Spirit/God's way of accepting humanity (Acts 15:10) and that they not burden the Gentile believers, "Since neither us nor our ancestors could keep the entire law" (Acts 15:10b). For me, the label "you Judaizers" contains a powerful terminology, which indicates several facts: that these teachers were present in the national council though they are not named. Not naming is again to show they were either losing face, and the church did not want to dishonour them in records; or, it could be interpreted that the Holy Spirit did not permit the Jerusalem Council to mention their names; or, St. Luke, the writer, was not allowed to do so by the Holy Spirit. Part of it is that James testified, "we did not send the Judaizers" (Acts 15:24). However, there is evidence in Pauline letters that such attitudes continued. Paul described them as "human pleasers" (Gal 6:12), "avoiding persecution" for the name of Christ (Gal 6:12) and "deliberate twisters of the truth" (Gal 1:7). Further, the church sends an ecumenical letter with Judas and Silas (Acts 15:22) embracing all the gentile believers. The Antioch church rejoices on receiving this letter (Acts 15:31). Thus, the early church is a pattern for us to discern principles of solidarity with newly converted families. But in which aspects can we trace consensus with the Holy Spirit at Ahamrai village?

Consensus with the Holy Spirit and Social Justice

Deuteronomy stipulates, "You must not convict anyone of a crime on the testimony of only one witness. The facts of the case must be established by the testimony of two or three witnesses" (Deut. 19:15; cf. Num. 35:30; Matt. 18:16; Jn 1:8; Acts 1:8 and 1 Jn 5:7). John the Evangelist clarifies the role of the Holy Spirit in mission as follows: "And when he comes, he will convict the world of its sin, and of God's righteousness, and of the coming judgment" (Jn 16:8). If that is the case, the Ahamrai event has more than three witnesses:

Firstly, the dying person's "last wish" for a Christian burial. Papi Reddy's last testament is the basis of the bereaved family's stand for the Christian funeral. As I see it, in this sense, Papi Reddy's last wish is considered a "Dying Declaration." It affirms biophily while we keep in mind Freire's warning of risks as part of the

---

[32] Jeremiah 31:31-34 talks about God himself *writing the law on human hearts*. It means "God alone can discern what is in an individual's heart." It bypasses the need for a priest/mediator, it goes beyond the need of written documents and protection of the law in the Ark. The circumcision of the heart is indicative of our mind, the organ of our memory, of ideas and the conscious decisions that we take. See Gerald L. Keown, Pamel L Scalise and Thomas G. Smothers et.al, *Word Biblical Commentary*, Vol. 27. (Dallas, TX: Word Books, 1995), 129-135.

biophilic journey.³³ For the family, it did not offer them smooth sailing in their faith pilgrimage, and the Patel clan's claim for caste burial tested them.

Secondly, the witness of three adult believers, namely Sara, the widow, Bhimsen, the son and Jayasheeli, the daughter-in-law: they testify to two realities: (i) that Papi Reddy truly believed Jesus as his personal saviour. When asked, Bhimsen clarified, "my father was on the sick bed, baptism does not validate his belief, and we are witnesses to his faith." The validity of his salvation is comparable to one of the criminals on the cross who repents. Affirming the thief's repentance, Jesus said, "I assure you, today you will be with me in paradise" (Lk 23:43). (ii) Bhimsen, Jayasheeli and Sara testify to Christ's healing power. Late D.G.S. Dinakaran of Chennai prayed for one of Bhimsen's young sons, who subsequently was healed of his chronic disease.

Thirdly, the witness of their spiritual father and the seminary team of forty to the faith of the family: the medical doctor (i) guided them to contact Dinakaran for healing prayers. And (ii) he requested the seminary authorities for moral support and to officiate at the funeral ceremony. The seminary team stood in solidarity with the bereaved family.

Fourthly, the Holy Spirit *confirms* their faith in Christ. In this sense, the Holy Spirit sows, nurtures and reaches out to humanity across caste, class, gender and national barriers. Consequently, all human support is secondary (the family, the spiritual father, the Patels and the seminarians). Humans are treated as Christ's partners in the Spirits' mission (1 Cor. 1:9).

Conclusion

I have presented a real-life example of inter-religious engagement in India. I have reflected on "church and social justice" with a focus on "consensus with the work of the Holy Spirit" in mission. In clarifying my thoughts, I have defined key terms, such as the church, social justice, consensus and *panchayat*. I have said that the church is a community of believers. The discussion is centred around the conflict over the funeral rite of Papi Reddy, who died on his sick bed as a believer in Christ. Should the family bury his body as a Christian or perform a Patel caste burial? It ended up in a Christian ceremony due to the unrelenting faith of the bereaved family. Consensus, for me, is a community hermeneutic. It means a general agreement on something most people share in a group.

My reflections also come from the Anabaptist seminary's engagement in conflict resolution. My thoughts concern functional justice and not a court judgment. For me, the Greek terms for justice, namely *krima* and *krino* imply both conflict resolution and solidarity with the bereaved family. I tested my concepts with those of Freire. Specifically, I use Freire's biophily in contrast to necrophily. Biophily honours solidarity with the common people. It means supporting the bereaved family in their new Christian faith. Necrophily, on the other hand, is a discourse that kills an individual's or community's self-affirmation. By self-affirmation, I refer to the family's experience of Christ. Freire points to three conversation partners in dialogue: the nostalgic religious

---

³³ Freire, *Pedagogy of the Oppressed*, 65.

rightists, the utopian leftists and the citizens. Freire advocates all three groups are necessary for a social revolution. But he advocates the third discourse model, explicitly *conscientazacao*, to raise the masses' critical conscience.

I then raised and answered the question of whether the Christian funeral at Ahamrai village was upon the testimony of two or three witnesses, as stipulated in Deuteronomy 19:15. There were, of course, more than three witnesses in this case. Firstly, it was the dead man's "dying declaration"; secondly, it was the "witness" of three adult believers; thirdly, we have the witness of their spiritual father and the forty-member seminary team. Finally, I argued that all human institutions are subject to testing whether they are in line with the person and work of the Holy Spirit (Acts 15:28).

Cooperation and Unity among the Mission Churches in Mizoram

H. Lalrinthanga

Ecumenism has undergone different understandings over the years. We can speak of three periods of the development of ecumenism. The first period is from the beginning of Christianity up till the first half of the twentieth century. During this period, because of the need for unity, ecumenism was understood as a cordial relationship of churches. From the second half of the twentieth century, the focus shifted to the inter-church dimension. During this period, there were cross-denominational contacts, though these did not go beyond the level of mutual understanding and cooperation. Thirdly, in the twenty-first century, ecumenism has been understood as a unity of all churches. The contemporary ecumenical movement has its roots in mission realities in the nineteenth and twentieth centuries. The deep desire for cooperation and the promotion of unity expressed at the World Missionary Conference at Edinburgh in 1910 represents a widespread practice of missionary cooperation that had developed in various parts of the world. This contribution will discuss cooperation and unity among the Presbyterian, Baptist and Evangelical missionaries in Mizoram that echoes the spirit of the IMC process.

European Missionary Enterprise in Mizoram

Three missionary societies entered Mizoram in the last decade of the nineteenth century and the beginning of the twentieth century: the Welsh Calvinistic Methodist Mission, the Baptist Missionary Society and the Lakher Pioneer Mission. These mission societies were very active in preaching the Gospel among the Mizo.

Welsh Calvinistic Methodist Mission

The first missionary of the Welsh Calvinistic Methodist Mission (later known as the Welsh Presbyterian Mission) was David Evan Jones. He grew up in a farmhouse called Bryn Melyn in Llandderfel, Merionethshire (now Gwynedd), Wales. While his father was a Presbyterian, his mother was an Anglican. He offered himself for mission work in 1888 and completed his theological training before arriving in Mizoram as a missionary.

Jones started his journey from Liverpool on June 26, 1897. When he reached Silchar, he was accompanied by T.J. Jones and a Khasi Christian teacher, Rai Bhajur and his wife, whom the Mission Board had appointed to help him. They arrived in Aizawl on August 31, 1897. Jones settled down in J.H. Lorrain and F.W. Savidge's (of the Arthington Aborigines Mission who had attempted to start mission work in the region in 1894) house on Tea-garden Hill. He benefited greatly from the experience and teaching of Lorrain and Savidge (whom the natives called *Pu Buanga* and *Sap Upa* respectively[1]), who helped him for four months.

The next year, Edwin Rowlands joined the group. Jones and Rowlands were very dissimilar in character and talents, but the one made up for the deficiencies of the other, and they worked well together. They worked tirelessly, spending much of their time preaching the Gospel, as J.M. Lloyd records,

> They made very extensive tours during the period 1899-1905. To the North they travelled up to the border of Manipur State, eastwards to Champhai which overlooks Burma, through thick jungle to the edge of Tripura State on the West, and to the South, which involved the longest journey of all. As they went, despite persistent opposition, they found a few willing listeners in almost every village.[2]

The first converts in the Lushai Hills (present-day Mizoram) were baptised on June 25, 1899, when two young men, Khuma and Khara, made formal confessions of their Christian faith.[3] The Welsh missionary work was divided into four branches: education, preaching, medical work and literature.[4] Presently, the Mizoram Presbyterian Church is the largest denomination in Mizoram. A 2020 statistic shows that there are 1141 local churches with 6,20,311 total members in the church.[5]

Baptist Missionary Society

In 1901, George Hughes, a missionary of the British Baptist Missionary Society (BMS) in Chittagong (in present day Bangladesh), urgently appealed to his mission headquarters to take the southern part of the Lushai hills as their mission field.[6] In the BMS report of 1901, Hughes wrote, "The great task of evangelising these accessible and loveable people is not beyond the power of our society to undertake. It is a privilege any society might covet without sin: an opportunity we should embrace without delay."[7] Subsequently, the BMS requested the Welsh mission "to transfer the southern portion of the Lushai Hills to their care."[8] According to Eleanor Bowser, before the coming of the BMS mission, some evangelists from Bengal attempted to work in the Lushai Hills, but the hardship

---

[1] Larrain was called *Pu Buanga,* meaning "Mr. Grey", for his grey hairs and Savidge was called *Sap Upa,* meaning "Old Mizo Sahib", as he was the older of the two.
[2] J. Meirion Lloyd, *History of the Church in Mizoram: Harvest in the Hills* (Aizawl: Synod Publication Board, 1991), 47.
[3] John Hughes Morris, *The Story of Our Foreign Mission: Presbyterian Church of Wales* (Aizawl: Synod Publication Board, 2003), 242.
[4] K. Thanzauva, *Reports of Foreign Mission of the Presbyterian Church of Wales on Mizoram, 1894-1957* (Aizawl: Synod Literature and Publication Board, 1997), 11.
[5] *Statistical Handbook Mizoram 2020* (Aizawl: Directorate of Economics and Statistics Government of Mizoram, 2021), 186.
[6] Lloyd, *History of the Church in Mizoram*, 74.
[7] *Reports by Missionaries of Baptist Missionary Society (BMS) 1901-1939* (Serkawn: Mizoram Gospel Centenary Committee, Baptist Church of Mizoram, 1993), 1.
[8] Donna Strom, *Wind through the Bamboo: The Story of Transformed Mizo*, reprint (Madras: Evangelical Literature Service, 1991), 33.

of the hills proved too much for them and they gave up. The BMS invited the Savidge and Lorrain, formerly of the Arthington Aborigenes Mission, to work in South Lushai for the BMS.[9]

Lorrain and Savidge arrived at Tlabung by boat on March 8, 1903, and were warmly welcomed by the church members at Sethlun under the leadership of Thankunga, who helped carry their luggage free of cost.[10] From Tlabung, they approached Lunglei and arrived on March 13, 1903.[11] There were 125 Christians belonging to 30 families at the time of the arrival of the Baptist mission.[12] They made Serkawn their mission station. They spent most of their first two years supervising the building work of the mission station. Lorrain and Savidge distributed the work among themselves: Savidge took charge of the school and Lorrain took responsibility of church matters. In his report of 1905, Lorrain reported the progress of their mission in South Lushai as follows:

> The Gospel Message is winning its way into the hearts and homes of these hardy hillsmen. This year our Evangelists have met with a much more kindly welcome in the distant villages than they did last year. Many have given up their charms and demon-worship and have thrown in their lot with the "Obeyers of God." Including their children, who are thus brought under Christian teaching, the new names on the Christian Register this year number 109.[13]

The Mizo Baptist Church is presently the second-largest denomination in Mizoram. There are 663 local churches with a total membership of 1,69,748.[14]

Lakher Pioneer Mission

In his book, *Five Years in Unknown Jungles for God and Empire*, Reginald A. Lorrain wrote of his ambition to become a missionary. He reported, "Returning to England in October 1902, with the firm intention of endeavouring to go forth into the Mission field should the way open, I did all in my power to persuade some Missionary society to send me forth."[15] Just then he received a letter from his elder brother, J.H. Lorrain, who, as mentioned earlier was working as a missionary at South Lushai. In the letter, his brother wrote about "the great needs of a wild tribe of head-hunting hillsmen which lay seven days journey south of their present station, and who were known as the Lakhers and for whom the Christian natives in Lushai had been very definitely praying for some time past, that a Missionary might be sent to tell these wild people of the Love of God and of his Son, Jesus Christ."[16] Feeling a definite divine call to evangelize the

---

[9] M. Eleanor Bowser, *Light on the Lushai Hills: The Story of a Dream that Came True* (London: The Carey Press, 1930), 11.
[10] P.L. Lianzuala, *Zofate Chanchin Tha Rawn Hlantute* (Lunglei: Joseph Lalhlimpuia, 2012), 319.
[11] H.W. Carter, *Chhim Bial Kohhran Chanchin* (Serkawn: author, 1945), 50.
[12] *Reports by Missionaries of Baptist Missionary Society.* 7.
[13] *Ibid.* 19.
[14] *Statistical Handbook of Mizoram 2020*, 186.
[15] Reginald A. Lorrain, *5 Years in Unknown Jungles* (Guwahati/Delhi: Spectrum Publications, 1988), 1-2.
[16] *Ibid.* 4.

Lakhers (also known as Mara), Lorrain approached the BMS in 1905 with a request to support him financially from the "Arthington funds" so that he might go to the Lakher land (Maraland). Unfortunately, his request was turned down. Nevertheless, Lorrain decided to go on his own, independent of any existing society trusting that God would give him the support he needed.[17]

Lorrain and his newly wedded wife left the cosmopolitan city of London on January 18, 1907. They arrived at Lunglei on March 5, 1907, where his brother was based, and stayed there for six months. On September 19, 1907, the Lorrains left for Saikao (Serkawr) in Maraland and arrived on September 26. On arrival, they met the village chief, who agreed to allow them to build their station in the village.

The first local church in Maraland was founded at Lorrain Ville, Saikao, in 1914 with missionaries and a few Lakher converts. Soon the number of Christians increased, requiring the need to establish more churches outside Lorrain Ville. The first local church with only native Lakher believers was established at Siaha in 1933. At present, there are 90 local churches with a total membership of 45,665.[18]

Cooperation and Unity among Mission Societies in Mizoram

In the 1910 Edinburgh conference, one of the eight volumes constituting the report of the conference bears the title, "Cooperation and the Promotion of Unity." It expresses a concern for missionary cooperation in the mission field. Though there may not be a direct relation between the International Missionary Council (IMC) and Mizoram, the missionary activities in the history of Christianity in Mizoram resonate with the discussions in the IMC process. The following discussions highlight some of the key areas of cooperation and unity among the mission churches in Mizoram.

1. Cordial Relationships

Mizoram in 1891 was under the colonial British. For administrative purposes, the region was divided into two districts – the North Lushai District and the South Lushai District. The division not only divided the land but the people and the church as well with the Welsh Calvinistic Methodist Mission working in The North Lushai Hill District was under the Baptist Missionary Society in the South Lushai District. With the presence of different missionary societies, denominational rivalries were very real among the churches. To create a cordial relationship, the then Superintendent of the Lushai Hills, Colonel John Shakespear invited missionaries both from the North and South districts to a meeting. Though no record of the meeting resolution was found, this meeting can be regarded as the starting point for cooperation and unity among the missionaries in the region. Lloyd writes, "No doubt, Shakespear emphasized the vital importance of ensuring the unity of the Mizo people, and the need of excluding denominationalism and its bitterness from the life of the growing

---

[17] *Ibid.* 5-6.
[18] *Statistical Handbook of Mizoram 2020*, 186.

church."[19] It is evident that there was a good relationship not only between the churches but also with the political administration in Mizoram. Jones, a Presbyterian missionary, said that the two mission societies were like two brothers. He writes of his Baptist counterpart, "They also cooperated well with us in North Mizoram and never allowed denominational differences to come between us."[20] C.L. Hminga assumes, "It will not be an exaggeration to say that the extent of cooperation between the two Missions has very few parallels in the history of the Christian mission."[21]

2. Acceptance of Ministry and Membership

As noted above, North Mizoram was under the Presbyterian church and South Mizoram was under the Baptist church. However, when people moved from North to South and vice versa, the relationship between Presbyterians and Baptists in Mizoram was such that there was no problem accepting the immigrant into each other's churches. Zairema writes, "A Baptist or a Presbyterian migrating to other area becomes automatically [a] member of the church in that area, no question arose concerning change of denomination."[22] He further writes, "Many of our people did not know to what denomination they belonged – they knew, however, that they were Christians and their duty is to spread the good news."[23] The BMS report of 1914 mentions the cordial relationship between the two mission churches as follows,

> The relations which exist between the Welsh Presbyterian Missionaries in the North Lushai Hills and ourselves of the Baptist Missionary Societies in the South are most happy and friendly. As the Lushais are so nomadic in their habits, it often happens that North Lushai Christians come South, and South Lushai Christians go North. The exchange is mutually beneficial. Although our modes of baptism differ, church members are transferred from one community to the other, according to the part of the country in which they happen to be living at the time. The Lushai Christians, both North and South, realize that they are all one in Christ Jesus.[24]

In the same vein, the assembly meeting of the Presbyterian church held in 1932 made the following resolution on the issue of accepting migrants into the membership of the church: "Full communicant member as full communicant members. Other non-full communicant members should accept according to the rules of a particular church. Infant baptism should be accepted as baptism."[25] Jones also writes, "When a Christian in one area (e.g., North) moved to another

---

[19] Lloyd, *History of the Church in Mizoram*, 77.
[20] D.E. Jones, *A Missionary's Autobiography*, trans. J.M. Lloyd (Aizawl: H. Liansailova, 1998), 42.
[21] C.L. Hminga, *The Life and Witness of the Churches in Mizoram* (Serkawn: Literature Committee, Baptist Church of Mizoram, 1987). 104.
[22] Zairema, *God's Miracle in Mizoram: A Glimpse of Christian Work Among Headhunters (Aizawl: Synod Press & Bookroom, 1978)*, 9.
[23] *Ibid.*
[24] *Reports by Missionaries of Baptist Missionary Society*, 117-118.
[25] H. Remthanga, *Synod Thurel Lakkhawm,* Vol. I, 1910-1950 (Aizawl: Synod Literature and Publication Board, 1996), 253.

area, he was given a letter of transfer and was assured of a welcome in his new home."[26]

A historic occasion that highlights the acceptance of each other's ministry by both churches was the ordination of the first Mizo Pastor. In 1913, at the autumn session of the presbytery, Chhuahkhama was ordained as a pastor, the first Mizo to be made so. Interestingly, the officiating minister in his ordination service was Rev. J.H. Lorrain, a Baptist missionary of the South. Jones, the then Presbyterian missionary, conferred the privilege of conducting this first act of ordination on his Baptist friend, whose ministry among the Mizo by that time had extended for nearly twenty years. So North and South, Baptist and Presbyterian rejoiced together in the act of comity not often equalled.[27]

3. Exchange of Fraternal Delegates

Hminga says that the Presbyterian and the Baptist churches in Mizoram started exchanging delegates to attend each other's presbyteries in 1919. However, this contradicts K.M.S. Dawngliana's statement in 1917, "Regular exchange of fraternal delegates between the Baptist Church in the South and the Presbyterian in the North started their annual council meetings."[28] The latter may be acceptable as the North presbytery meeting of 1916 resolved to send fraternal delegates to the presbytery of the Baptist church for the first time in the history of the church in Mizoram.[29] Hauchunga and Dohnuna attended the Baptist presbytery in 1917.

The practice of exchanging fraternal delegates was later extended to the third church body in the region, the Lakher church. The Baptist Church of Mizoram sent two fraternal delegates to the first Presbytery meeting of the Lakher church at Serkawr.[30] In the 1960s, Hrathu Nohro wrote a letter to the Presbyterian church on behalf of the Lakher Independent Evangelical Church (LIEC) requesting the exchange of delegates to each other's presbytery meetings. The Standing Committee of the Presbyterian church decided that the LIEC may send delegates to the synod meeting in 1962 and that the two churches would discuss the exchange of delegates later.[31] Since then, the Presbyterian church and the Lakher church have exchanged fraternal delegates to their synods and assemblies, respectively. Inter-communion with the Lakher church started at a much later date.[32] Through these fraternal exchanges, the churches in the region are learning and borrowing ideas from one another.

---

[26] Jones, *A Missionary's Autobiography*, 42.
[27] Lloyd, *History of the Church in Mizoram*, 164.
[28] K.M.S. Dawngliana, "Important Events of BCM," in *Compendium* (Lunglei: The Centenary Committee, Baptist Church of Mizoram, 2003), 222.
[29] "Presbytery October 1916, No. 12," in H. Remthanga, *Synod Thurel Lak Khawm*, Vol. I, 1910-1950 (Aizawl: Synod Literature and Publication Board, 1996), 252.
[30] Dawngliana, "Important Events of BCM," 225.
[31] "Standing Committee 6.11.1962, No. 8," in H. Remthanga, *Synod Thurel Lak Khawm*, Vol. II, 1951-1970 (Aizawl: Synod Literature and Publication Board, 1998), 292.
[32] Hminga, *The Life and Witness of the Churches in Mizoram*, 282.

4. Bible Translation

The missionary societies also worked together towards promoting Christian literature. In 1895, Lorrain and Savidge began translating the Bible into Mizo. In 1897, when Lorrain and Savidge left Mizoram, the Presbyterian missionaries, Jones and Rowlands took over the translation work. In 1903, when Lorrain and Savidge returned to Mizoram as Baptist missionaries, they helped the Presbyterian missionaries in revising the drafts. The missionaries, irrespective of their denominational affiliations, were committed to the great task of completing the translation of the whole of the Bible into Mizo. The translation of the whole New Testament to Mizo was completed in 1916. In his report of 1916-17, Jones says, "We rejoice with the South brethren on the completion of the New Testament in Lushai."[33] Lloyd remarks on the good cooperation of the North and South in translation works,

> Although the Baptist and Presbyterian mission centres at Serkawn (Lunglei) and Aizawl stood at a considerable distance from each other, a matter of eight days journey along the Government path, the two missions always worked well together. The sphere of Bible translation has in the past been a notoriously delicate one a peculiarly liable to cause disagreement between missions of different denominations ... From the first, however, though there were minor problems and disagreements there was constant cooperation between North and South. In time they worked out a complete programme for the translation work and Lorrain acted as general editor in liaison with the Bible Society.[34]

Lorrain captures the spirit of cooperation and appreciation with which the two missions worked in the translation project when he states: "Since then, thanks very largely to the labours and cooperation of the Welsh Missionaries who followed us in North Lushai, our people have now quite an assortment of useful literature in their language."[35]

After the publication of the New Testament, they continued the translation of the Old Testament, and by the time Lorrain left Mizoram in 1932, the translation was almost complete. The missionaries from the North and South divided the portions of the Bible translation and exchanged whatever they had finished for editing.[36] The translation of the Old Testament was completed in 1956., The complete Mizo Bible finally came out In 1959, and the Mizo finally had the whole Bible in their language.[37] It was a joint venture of the Presbyterian church and the Baptist church which saw close cooperation between the two missions from the stat till the completion of the translation work. According to Zaihmingthanga, the Mizo Christians loved the Mizo Bible, but only a few could

---

[33] Thanzauva, *Reports of Foreign Mission of the Presbyterian Church of Wales on Mizoram*, 61.
[34] Lloyd, *History of the Church in Mizoram*, 131.
[35] *Reports by Missionaries of Baptist Missionary Society*, 128.
[36] *Kohhran Inpumkhatna Inzirtirna* (Aizawl: Mizoram Presbyterian Kohhran, 2018), 12-13.
[37] B. Lalthangliana, *India, Burma leh Bangladesh-a Mizo Kohhrante* (Aizawl: Remkungi, 2007), 344.

get hold of the Bible since only 5000 copies were printed. Thousands of Mizo Christians were disappointed at not having a chance to have one at home.[38]

Over time there was a desire to revise the Mizo Bible. Rev. Liangkhaia, a Presbyterian pastor, was requested to look into the revision of the Gospel of Matthew. A team comprising of five members from the Baptist church and seven members from the Presbyterian church was appointed to review the translation at the District Council Hostel in August 1964, with Rev. Zairema, a Presbyterian pastor acting as the Secretary. The Bible Society of India approved the nominated members from the Presbyterian and Baptist churches. In 1982 Rev. Zairema was appointed a full-time worker to look after the translation and designated "Chief Translator". The committee met almost every month to edit the translation. The New Testament revision was completed in 1984. Rev. Zairema of the Presbyterian church and Rev. Chalbuanga of the Baptist church spent two months proofreading the revision before it was printed. The New Testament revision came out at the end of 1986, and the Bible Society of India aptly named it *"Hmangaihna Aw"* (The Voice of Love).

After completing the New Testament translation, a Draft Committee was formed for the Old Testament revision. Since some of the appointed members were busy looking after their pastorates, Rev. H.S. Luaia and Rev. Chalbuanga, both of the Baptist church, and Rev. Lalthanga and Rev. Lalruma, both of the Presbyterian church, were entrusted with take care of the revision. They spent at least ten days every month working on the revision. The Old Testament revision was completed in 1992. The second edition of the whole Bible was printed in November 1995.[39]

5. Production of a Christian Hymn Book

The Mizo love singing, and it made up a major part of their social life even before the arrival of Christianity. When they became Christians, singing continued to play a key role in the church. Knowing their desire to learn songs, Jones compiled a small collection of hymns, and the Mizo eagerly bought this little songbook when it came out.[40] This small hymn book was expanded after the arrival of Rowlands in 1898, who translated and composed over a hundred hymns, of which 90 are still in Mizo hymnody today. He is remembered for his gift of singing and composing hymns.[41] The second hymn book containing 83 hymns was published in 1903 at the Allahabad Mission Press by the North India Christian Tract and Book Society. It was republished within a year or two with the addition of 42 hymns. In 1909, an enlarged edition of the Mizo hymn book was conjointly published by the Presbyterian and the Baptist missions. This new

---

[38] Zaihmingthanga, *The History of Christianity in Mizoram, 1944-1994* (Aizawl: Lengchhawn Press, 2016), 54.
[39] Lalthangliana, *India, Burma leh Bangladesh-a Mizo Kohhrante*, 344-346.
[40] Thanzauva, *Reports of Foreign Mission of the Presbyterian Church of Wales on Mizoram*, 9.
[41] C. Hrangdula, "Music Ministry," in *Compendium* (Lunglei: The Centenary Committee, Baptist Church of Mizoram, 2003), 176.

hymn book contained 273 hymns, including a few new hymns by Lorrain and Savidge.[42] In the Report of the Lushai Hills, 1908-1909, Robert Evans writes,

> I feel thanks to God that the Baptist missionaries in Lungleh are such openhearted and godly men. We and they are able to work together in perfect harmony. Sometimes we hold united meetings; the Hymn Books and tune-books of both Missions are one and the same, and the Tonic Solfa has been adopted by both. We believe that this unity and harmony will bear much fruit in the future.[43]

This is true of South Mizoram as well, as Lorrain writes, "The Tonic Solfa System having been taught by the Welsh Missionaries to the Christians in North Lushai, our people got a liking for it, and we felt it best to accede to their wishes and let them learn that system instead."[44] Since then, the Presbyterian church and the Baptist church have always worked together in bringing out later editions of the Mizo hymn book.

The third Mizo revival, which took place in 1913, was very important for the development of the Mizo Christian hymn book. After the revival, there was an improvement in both the translated hymns and hymns composed by the Mizo. The third edition of the Mizo hymn book, containing 450 hymns, was published in 1914. Of the 450 hymns, 193 were either composed or translated by Mizo Christians. Around 10,000 copies were printed.[45] Later, more hymns were added by Lorrain, Savidge, Jones and Rowlands. By 1927, there were about 500 hymns in the hymn book.[46] The centenary edition of the hymn book was published in 1944 and had as many as 537 hymns.

After the joint conference of the Presbyterian church and Baptist church in 1949, the Mizo hymn book was revised, and the first music edition with the tonic solfa notations was published in 1957. As a result of this addition, the edition was greatly welcomed everywhere.[47] The two churches again jointly published a revised edition in 1986. The meeting of the joint committee of the two churches held at Aizawl on July 23, 2002, decided to revise and enlarge the hymn book once again.[48] This edition was published in 2004. This new Christian hymn book contained 600 songs; 43 songs in the old hymn book were dropped, and 106 new hymns were added.[49] From the beginning, the music committees of both the Presbyterian and Baptist churches worked together in preparing the hymn book, which was then published by the Synod Literature and Publication Board.

6. Publication of the Christian Herald

In traditional Mizo society, every village had its *Tlangau* or crier. He was one of the most important village officials and was responsible for proclaiming the

---

[42] *Reports by Missionaries of Baptist Missionary Society*, 52.
[43] Thanzauva, *Reports of Foreign Mission of the Presbyterian Church of Wales on Mizoram*, 37.
[44] *Reports by Missionaries of Baptist Missionary Society*, 53.
[45] *Ibid.* 129.
[46] Jones, *A Missionary's Autobiography*, 59.
[47] Hrangdula, "Music Ministry," 178.
[48] *Ibid.*
[49] *Secretary's Report 2004 in 2004 Synod Bu* (Aizawl: The Mizoram Presbyterian Church, 2004), 162.

chief's orders to the village. When the Chief wanted to make an announcement, he would send the *Tlangau* out to the village, who would then go around the village proclaiming the chief's orders. Christian mission in Mizoram appropriated this use of the tradition of the *Tlangau* with the publication of a magazine called *Krista Tlangau*, meaning "Herald of Christ".

The first issue of the magazine was published in October 1911 by the North Mizo church under the title *Kristian Tlangau* ("Christian Herald"). Though it was published by the North, the South missionaries also benefitted from this magazine. Lorrain writes in his report of 1913, "Our South Lushai Christians send articles to it for publication. Over 80 copies come to me alone every month for my Sunday School teachers and others. The subscription is twelve annas per annum."[50] All the important resolutions of the presbyteries of the South were also published in *Kristian Tlangau* before the Baptist church had its own official organ, *Kohhran Beng*, which began publications in 1947.[51]

According to Lloyd, the *Kristian Tlangau* had been fully accepted as the Christian monthly magazine, had a very wide circulation, and was read by many outside the confines of the Mizo Hills. Sermons were also included as part of the regular monthly content. Furthermore, *Kristian Tlangau* always contained news and reflections on the death of prominent Mizo Christians. These were read with interest as they were potted biographies. Later the magazine began to include a surprisingly varied and up-to-date account of Christian news worldwide.[52] Despite a few inconveniences in the past, it is regularly published even today, and the number of copies in circulation were at 43,000 in 2021.

Conclusion

This discussion indicates a cordial and close relationship among the Mizoram Presbyterian Church, the Baptist Church of Mizoram and the Evangelical Church of Mizoram in the initial period of the history of Christianity in Mizoram. Cooperation among the mission churches in the translation of the Bible, the publishing of the Mizo hymn book and the exchange of delegation in each other's Presbytery meetings were remarkable acts of ecumenicity among the Mizo Christians. There is no doubt that the spirit of cooperation and unity among the mission societies in Mizoram resonates with what was being discussed in the IMC process.

---

[50] *Reports by Missionaries of Baptist Missionary Society*, 107.
[51] C. Rothuama, "Communications in the Baptist Church of Mizoram," in *Compendium* (Lunglei: The Centenary Committee, Baptist Church of Mizoram, 2003), 170.
[52] Lloyd, *History of the Church in Mizoram*, 244- 245.

Ecumenical Continuity of Missions: The Working Principles and Objectives of the International Missionary Council and the Lairam Isua Krista Baptist Kohhran

Zadingluaia Chinzah

A pertinent challenge that emerges in understanding the influence of the International Missionary Council (IMC), a Council that no longer exists on its own, on an ecclesial body in a distant corner of Mizoram, Northeast India, is challenging and intriguing. This contribution attempts to respond to this pertinent challenge by examining the ecumenical continuity in Christian missions at Lawngtlai, Mizoram, leading to the formation of the Lairam Isua Krista Baptist Kohhran (LIKBK, Lairam Jesus Christ Baptist Church) in 1999. What is the relation between the event at Lawngtlai, Mizoram, 1999, and the event at Lake Mohonk, New York, 1921? Lake Mohonk gave the world an ecumenical endeavour (the International Missionary Council), whereas Lawngtlai 1999 became the birthplace of a successful attempt at an organic union (the formation of an ecumenical ecclesiastical body, the LIKBK). These historic events are not only separated by an extensive geographical hiatus but are chronologically more than half a century apart. To understand the rubrics that relate the two seemingly unrelated events, it is imperative to be boldly assertive in deliberating "ecumenism" as the common ground on which these two connect and interlace. A cursory glance at the ecumenicity of the IMC, a general overview of the genesis and proceedings leading to the development of the LIKBK, and its relationship with the IMC through its principles and objectives of missions will be highlighted in this undertaking.

Ecumenical/Ecumenism: History, Meaning and Concern

Ecumenism (as a noun) or ecumenical (as an adjective) are derived from the Greek word *oikoumene,* which means the whole inhabited world or the Roman world. Norman Goodall explicates *oikoumene* as deeply rooted in the Greek, Roman and Christian civilization.[1] Goodall enunciates further that the term *oikoumene* has been repeatedly redefined, wherein *oikoumene* became a vocabulary related to the worldwide ecumenical movement that endeavours Christian unity. Ecumenism did not emerge abruptly. The movement for ecumenism through the Pietistic movement, Evangelical Awakening,

---

[1] Norman Goodall, *The Ecumenical Movement: What it Is and What It Does* (London: Oxford University Press, 1961), 3.

Evangelical Alliance, Students' Movements and rise of Mission Societies were precursors to the resurgence of the ecumenism of the early Church's Ecumenical Councils convened at Nicaea, Constantinople, Ephesus and Chalcedon. The spirit and praxis of ecumenism were practically conspicuous in these early Church's Ecumenical Councils, which endeavoured to solve faith questions and produce common creeds. O.L. Snaitang highlights the various emphasis ecumenism/ecumenical takes into consideration: issues about unity and missions, the union of churches, dialogue with other faiths and ideologies, solidarity with victims of injustice and integrity of creation.[2] Gradually, ecumenism became the movement in which Christians from different denominations worked together to develop closer relationships to promote Christian unity and work towards the evangelization of the inhabited world.

The Formation of the International Missionary Council

History was made at Edinburgh in 1910 by hosting, proceeding and deliberating a World Missionary Council representing, as far as possible, members of different Christian churches and mission societies. It was an ecumenical gathering. Among the various concerns raised at Edinburgh 1910, one of the major topics was mission cooperation and the promotion of unity. To continue the ecumenical miracle of Edinburgh 1910, the Continuation Committee and Emergency Committee was formed. John R. Mott, Joseph H. Oldham and Nathan Soderblom were ecumenically inspired leaders who travelled the world spreading the message of the importance of unity and cooperation in addition to the publication of the *International Review of Mission*. The efforts of these committees and leaders led to the formation of the International Missionary Council.

Lake Mohonk, New York, was the arena in which the world saw and understood the necessity of unity in mission through the founding of the IMC in October 1921. It was the practical execution of the suggestion to form an international missionary council based on national cooperative agencies deliberated at Edinburgh 1910.[3] The IMC became the extension of the ecumenical movement envisaged at Edinburgh. It was founded on three principles that reflected immense practical experiences. The first principle enunciates that "the only bodies entitled to determine missionary policy are the missionary societies and boards, or the churches which they represent, and the churches in the mission field."[4] T.V. Philip remarks that the IMC is "an institution that stood for the recognition of the inseparability of unity and mission

---

[2] O.L. Snaitang, *A History of Ecumenical Movement: An Introduction* (Bangalore: BTESSC/SATHRI, 2004), 13-15.
[3] Willian Richey Hogg, *Ecumenical Foundations: A History of the International Missionary Council and its Nineteenth-Century Background* (New York: Harper and Brothers Publishers, 1952), 202.
[4] *Ibid*, 204.

within the ecumenical movement."⁵ This principle reflects that churches and Christian missions could no longer be separate in evangelism. It endeavours that churches take an active role in mission activities, especially in contributing to the evangelisation of the world.

The second principle enunciates "that no statement should be issued on any matter involving an ecclesiastical or doctrinal question, on which the members of the Council or bodies constituting the Council may differ."⁶ This principle is derivative of an experience in Christian history where differences in doctrine/faith interpretation had resulted in an uncalled division of both the disciples of Christ and the church, which is the body of Christ. It purports a theological basis of cooperation by recognizing the detrimental consequences of matters concerning the interpretation of faith, usually centred on doctrines.

The third principle is the recognition that the successful working of the IMC "is entirely dependent on the gift of God of the spirit of fellowship, mutual understanding and desire to cooperate."⁷ It recognizes that mutuality and cooperation can and will continue to exist without being sceptical and critical about doctrinal differences. This last principle is a testimony that unity, an essential component of the IMC's successful working and achievements, rests not on the whims and fancies of individuals and their objective aspirations. The reliance on the gift of God makes the IMC an ecumenical endeavour that envisages evangelism of the world as a unified effort. A cumulative understanding of the principles of the IMC highlights its vision of bringing together national Christian councils to a shared sense of unity for a united effort in world evangelisation⁸ and taking up the goal of planting indigenous churches.⁹

Kenneth Scott Latourette enumerates the function of the IMC as being,
- to stimulate thinking and investigation,
- to make the results available for all missionary societies and missions,
- to help coordinate the activities of the national missionary organizations of the different countries and of the societies they represent,
- to bring about united action where necessary in missionary matters,
- to help unite Christian public opinion in support of freedom of conscience and religion and of missionary liberty,
- to help unite the Christian forces of the world in seeking justice in international and inter-racial relations,
- to be responsible for the publication of *The International Review of Missions* and such other publications as in the judgment of the Council may contribute to the study of missionary questions, and

---

⁵ T.V. Philip, *Edinburgh to Salvador Twentieth Century Ecumenical Missiology: A Historical Study of the Ecumenical Discussions on Mission* (Delhi & Tiruvalla: ISPCK & CSS, 1999), 55.
⁶ Hogg, *Ecumenical Foundations*, 204.
⁷ *Ibid.* 205.
⁸ Snaitang, *A History of Ecumenical Movement*, 108.
⁹ Hogg, *Ecumenical Foundations*, 207.

- to call a world missionary conference if and when this should be deemed desirable.[10]

Ecumenical concerns and issues of the IMC are conspicuous in its understanding of "cooperation". Issues which raised questions such as "Is uniformity of belief essential to missionary cooperation?" "Is any cooperation possible with doctrinal differences?" and "Does the International Missionary Council not constitute a super-board imposing doctrinal restrictions?"[11] were seen as relevant and practical. Deliberations were made to recognise the importance of a common obligation of evangelizing the world instead of dwelling on doctrinal matters. The IMC recognised that doctrinal differences had not hindered cooperation in counsel because "gathered together, we have experienced a growing unity among ourselves, in which we recognised the influence of the Holy Spirit."[12] The IMC stated that "it would be entirely out of harmony with the spirit of this movement to press for such cooperation in work as would be felt to compromise doctrinal principles or to strain conscience."[13] The recognition of the maxim "doctrine divides" was understood, emphasised and evaluated in the preliminary stage of the formation and development of the IMC.

The Formation of the Lairam Isua Krista Baptist Kohhran and its Mission Objectives

The Lai people inhabit the Lawngtlai district of Mizoram in Northeast India. A substantial percentage of their population is dispersed in various parts of Mizoram and the Chin state of Myanmar. They are culturally distinct from the other ethnic tribes of Mizoram. The Lai people are divided into various subtribes. The recognition and identification of their distinct ethnicity were cemented by the Government of India, which granted them the Lai Autonomous District Council in 1972 on the premise of the distinctiveness of identity. The working and execution of the Autonomous District Council resulted in the resurgence of ethnic consciousness leading to the formation of two indigenous churches, that

---

[10] Kenneth Scott Latourette, "Ecumenical Bearings of the Missionary Movement and the International Missionary Council," in *A History of the Ecumenical Movement*, Vol. 1, eds. Ruth Rouse and Stephen Charles Neill (Geneva: World Council of Churches, 1953), 367.
[11] Hogg, *Ecumenical Foundations*, 216.
[12] *Ibid.* 217.
[13] *Ibid.* 218.

is, the Isua Krista Kohhran (IKK, Church of Jesus Christ) in 1970[14] and the Lairam Baptist Kohhran (LBK, Lairam Baptist Church) in 1982.[15]

Apart from political development, other factors propelled the formation of IKK and LBK. Among the various factors, the evangelistic zeal of propagating the Gospel to their own ethnic group outside Mizoram, especially those living in Myanmar, was self-assertive missionary zeal.[16] Another factor was the recognition of being discriminated against by their parent Baptist Church of Mizoram,[17] where discrimination was conspicuous in employment, opportunities in technical education and pastoral care. The third factor was the desire to advance and preserve the Lai cultural identity.[18]

Although the movement for an independent church body for the Lai people within their own confined area had already existed from the beginning of the 1960s, it was realized only on May 23, 1970, with the formation of the IKK in a convention at Rawlbuk, where representatives from different churches within the Lai area were present. It must be noted that breaking away without the consent of their mother church, the Mizoram Baptist Church (MBC), was never the intention of the Lai church leaders. They desired to stay connected with the MBC through affiliation. However, when the MBC refused their request, the only option before the Lai people was to establish an independent church.

The formation of the LBK was the second movement for an independent Lai church. Due to certain differences, some of the Lai people could not join the IKK. The LBK was formed a decade later, on January 7, 1982. The founders of the LBK had requested the Mizoram Baptist Church to depute one pastor for the position of General Secretary for two years. They also suggested that the new church would continue to give the mission fund to the headquarters, collaborate in the fields of literature, the Sunday school and the book room (till the new church could establish these departments on its own), continue to have MBC pastors in the Lai area (till the new church made new appointments), and permission to be given to Lai pastors under the MBC to join the new church. However, the request was denied by the MBC leadership. Subsequently, the Lai churches broke away from the MBC and formed the LBC.

---

[14] See V. Suikharliana, "An Appraisal of the Lairam Jesus Christ Baptist Church's Understanding of Mission in the Light of Mission Dei" (Master of Theology diss., Aizawl Theological College, 2012), 9-10. See also Raldawna. *Isua Krista Kohhran Tobul* (Origin of Church of Jesus Christ), (Lawngtlai: IKK Press, 1994); J.H.Chinzah, "The Lai People's Search for Political and Ecclesiastical Autonomy" (Master of Theology diss., United Theological College, 2000).
[15] Lalmuankima. *In His Service* (Lawngtlai: The Publication Board of Lairam Baptist Church, 1997); See also, Chinzah. "The Lai People's Search for Political and Ecclesiastical Autonomy" in *Souvenir of Lairam Baptist Church: Centenary Publication* (Lawngtlai: The Centenary Committee, Lairam Baptist Church, 1994).
[16] Raldawna, *Isua Krista Kohhran Tobul,* 13–14.
[17] Lalmuankima, *In His Service*, 30.
[18] B. Lalramzama, "An Evaluation of the Missiological Motives and Objectives of the Lai Churches in Mizoram" (Master of Theology diss., United Theology College, 2003), 20.

The two indigenous Lai churches operated and functioned separately for nearly two decades. Realising that both churches were formed with similar motives and objectives, sparks of desire to merge into a unified ecclesial body were sporadically ignited among the theological graduates (Pastors and Probationary Pastors), lay leaders (Elders and Deacons) and the general public belonging to the two indigenous church bodies. Gradually, a commitment evolved among the Lai churches that missionary zeal and ecclesial autonomy could be attained, strengthened and enlarged by the coming together of the two Lai churches into an organic union. Thus, the realisation of ethnic consciousness coupled with belongingness to the same faith and a commitment to evangelisation evolved into an ecumenical endeavour that started the negotiations for organic unity between the two indigenous churches.

Organic Union and the Lairam Isua Krista Baptist Kohhran

In the wake of the ecumenical movement propelled by the evangelical awakening, churches in the world gradually began to think of ways in which different churches could be united. Churches of the same doctrinal background began comprehending the importance of uniting in various forms. To better understand the church union of the Lai churches, it would be relevant to mention here the various models of Church unity: organic, conciliar, spiritual and federal unions.[19] The one that is much sought after by denominations or churches negotiating for unity is the "organic union," which is a Biblical ideal inspired by St. Paul's favourite description of the church as the body of Christ.[20] This model's uniqueness and beauty are that it envisions a unity of doctrine, ministry and understanding of the sacraments and of polity, that is, having a common organizational structure.[21] Such a union involves a complete merger of the uniting churches in which structural identities and names are surrendered for a singular structure and name. V.V. Thomas summarises organic unity as a "description of a condition where divided churches come together to form a new fellowship with a new identity."[22]

Leslie Newbegin remarks, "the final and terrible difficulty is that Churches cannot unite unless they are willing to die."[23] Stephen Neill also notes that for an organic union to succeed, it has to be supported by various theologians,

---

[19] Snaitang, *A History of Ecumenical Movement*, 79-84; Frederick F. Downs, "Models of Church Unity," in *Essays on Christianity in North East India*, eds. Milton S. Sangma & David R. Syiemlieh (Delhi: ISPCK, 1994), 263.
[20] *Experiments in Christian Unity: A National Council of Churches in India Booklet* (Delhi: ISPCK, 1983), 43.
[21] *Experiments in Christian Unity*, 43.
[22] V.V. Thomas, "Historical Models of Church Unity," in *History of Ecumenical Movement: Issues, Challenges and Perspectives*, comp. Watimongla Jamir (Kolkata: SCEPTRE, 2014), 209.
[23] Lesslie Newbegin, "Organic Union," in *Dictionary of the Ecumenical Movement*, ed. Nicholas Lossky (Geneva: WCC, 1991), 1028.

international church leaders and uniting churches to make it fruitful.[24] Taking into consideration the statements made by Newbegin and Neill, the movement towards an organic unity by the Lai people from the two indigenous churches, IKK and LBK, affirms that organic union is possible when churches surrender both their theological and non-theological differences and are willing to lose all their previous identities. This organic unity between the two churches may also be regarded as an ecumenical endeavour that is both historic and the work of the spirit of God, reflecting the third principle of the IMC.

Several issues needed to be resolved in bringing about the merger of the IKK and the LBK. Concerns regarding the location of its headquarters, the future of their alliances with other partners in mission, and the leadership positions were difficult questions that needed to be addressed. However, acknowledging the far-reaching consequences of an organic union, the church leaders comprising of theologians and lay elders continued their dialogue for unification. Consequently, in 1995, the negotiating churches' assemblies unanimously decided to welcome the proposal and carry on the dialogue towards organic unity.[25] Both the churches collaborated to form the Churches Unity Commission (CUC) as a mediating body comprising delegates from both church assemblies. The commission included (i) office bearers of both churches; (ii) pastors and probationary pastors; (iii) evangelists from both churches; (iv) all elders from both churches with three deacons from all local churches; and (v) one youth and women delegates each from local churches.[26]

The negotiations for unity are not efforts that immediately bear success. It was only after several attempts at negotiations that the assemblies of the IKK and the LBC voted in favour of unification in 1997 and 1998, respectively. The CUC also suggested that the assemblies encourage mutual cooperation and understanding through conducting seminars and joint fellowships/conferences to speed up the CUC also proposed: (i) to realise the unification before 2000 AD and (ii) to convene a Special Joint Assembly (SJA) to declare the unification.[27] The above proposals were discussed and approved by both assemblies in 1999. Both assemblies agreed to convene the SJA on November 25-28, 1999. There was unanimity in affirming the SJA as the competent body for matters considering: (i) its actual representation of the full-fledged assembly members, (ii) its constitutional provision and (iii) its delegation of power and function.[28]

Out of several options, it was voted to name the unified church Isua Krista Kohhran Lairam. In the annual Assembly held on March 28, 2003, the name of

---

[24] Stephen Charles Neill, "Plans of Union and Reunion 1910-1948," in *A History of the Ecumenical Movement 1517-1948*, Vol. I, eds. Ruth Rouse and S.C. Neill (Geneva: WCC, 1953), 449.
[25] Vanlalzauva, "How It Has Happened: Ecumenical Movement and Its Success in Lairam," in *Church Union Souvenir* (Lawngtlai: IKKL, 2000), 81.
[26] C. Hrangzuala, *Ka Luah Hian Hriak i Thih a*, Vol. I (Lawngtlai: Author, 2014), 156.
[27] Vanlalzauva, "How It Has Happened: Ecumenical Movement and Its Success in Lairam," 81.
[28] *Ibid.* 82.

the church was changed to Lairam Isua Krista Baptist Kohhran (LIKBK)[29]. The LIKBK was formed with the following mission statement and objectives stated in its Constitution:

> The basis of the Lairam Jesus Christ Baptist Church is the establishment of God's Kingdom on earth. The church was founded with the primary purpose that through its ministry, God's Kingdom will be inaugurated, made to grow and emerge with ever greater clarity. The Lairam Jesus Christ Baptist Church believes that God has called all the Lai people within and outside the boundaries of the Lai Autonomous District Council to be his people and serve him in unity.[30]

On completion of this organic union, the LIKBK had innumerable administrative structuring to look into since both the IKK and LBK merged to form a wholly new ecclesial institution: the drawing up of the Church constitution and byelaws, selection of its headquarters, the functioning and administration of various departments of the new body and so on.

The LIKBK is a member of the Baptist World Alliance, Asian Baptist Federation, Council of Baptist Churches in Northeast India, Mizoram Baptist Federation, Global Council of Chin Fellowship, Global Alliance of Chin Churches and Chin Baptist Churches-USA. Regionally, it is in a dialogical relationship with the Presbyterian Church of India, Mizoram Synod, Baptist Church of Mizoram and the Evangelical Church of Maraland. The LIKBK also cooperates with mission societies such as Serving in Mission-North East India, Youth with a Mission, Churches Auxiliary for Social Action and World Vision in propagating the social aspect of the Gospel.

The LIKBK continues the mission work in fields previously under the IKK and the LBK. It continues the Home Mission work, which concentrates heavily on the Bru and Chakma areas. Mission work also continues in Manipur (among the Meitei, Vaiphei and Lamkang) and the Mising ethnic groups in Dhemaji, Assam. In 2012, the LIKBK adopted Odisha as a mission field. The LIKBK also has foreign mission fields in Myanmar and Bangladesh. The LIKBK mission involvement includes evangelism, school education, literature and films. On the social aspect of missions, the LIKBK is involved in medical work, rehabilitation of drug users (Rescue Home) and adoption centres for orphans.

International Missionary Council Meetings and its Concerns

The Jerusalem Council of the IMC, 1928, recognised the threat of secularism to Christianity.[31] It also marked a turning point in the conception of Christian missions from being viewed as the foreign activities of Western churches to a larger view and understanding of Christian missions as a partnership and full cooperation between the older churches and the younger churches. It led to a

---

[29] Lairam Isua Krista Baptist Kohhran, *Minutes of the Meeting of Annual Assembly* (March, 2003), 6.
[30] *Constitution & Bye Laws of Lairam Jesus Christ Baptist Church* (Lawngtlai: Assembly of Lairam Jesus Christ Baptist Church, 2011), 2-4.
[31] Latourette, "Ecumenical Bearings of the Missionary Movement and the International Missionary Council," 369.

"church-centric" approach where the indigenous church was the focal centre for planning and action.³² At Jerusalem, the reality of the church in the mission field forced the missionary movement to take the "church" seriously in its thinking.³³ The rapid spread of younger churches led by rising competent leaders was a historical fact Jerusalem 1928 could no longer ignore. Jerusalem 1928 also emphasised the social dimension of the Christian message. The centrality of Christ, partnership and the recognition of the universality of secularism stimulated an innovative evangelistic impulse.³⁴

The IMC of Tambaram 1938 became a meeting of churches, which addressed issues on confrontations with other religions.³⁵ It saw the church as the supreme agent of unity for evangelising. It also expressed the conviction that effective evangelization was possible through unity and cooperation. The five main subjects at Tambaram 1938 were (i) the faith by which the church lives, (ii) the relation of Christian witness to non-Christian religions and cultures and the work of evangelism, (iii) the life and work of the church, (iv) the environment of the Church and (v) cooperation and unity.³⁶ Church-centric issues became more prominent in mission activities. It demonstrated the strength of the younger churches, where recognition of the younger churches to support, govern and propagate themselves – an approach which was a new dimension to missionary thinking.³⁷ The IMC of Tambaram 1938 also added a fourth dimension to the missionary movement, the economic and social environment (in addition to evangelistic, educational and medical enterprises).³⁸

Whitby 1947 developed a theology of partnership in mission. It proclaimed "Christian Witness in a Revolutionary World," where delegates faced a threefold task: surveying the effects of war upon the church, re-discovering the essential Gospel and its relevance for a broken world and calling the church again to its central task – evangelism.³⁹ The significance of Whitby 1947 is its determination to make evangelism the heart and core of the missionary movement; its revelation of a new equality, a new oneness, between younger and older churches; and its demonstration of the high unity of the Protestant world Christian community.⁴⁰ Renewed emphasis on Christian fellowship and unity was undertaken, with "Partnership in Mission" being a serious concern. It realised the vision of Edinburgh 1910, "partnership in obedience" to the Great Commission. "Partnership in obedience" expressed the idea that the task of mission is a global task and is to be understood in partnership based on common faith and obedience.⁴¹

---

[32] Hogg, *Ecumenical Foundation*, 254.
[33] Philip, *Edinburgh to Salvador*, 34.
[34] Hogg, *Ecumenical Foundations*, 257-58.
[35] *Ibid.* 296.
[36] Snaitang, *A History of Ecumenical Movement*, 110.
[37] Philip, *Edinburgh to Salvador*, 38.
[38] Hogg, *Ecumenical Foundations*, 299.
[39] *Ibid.* 336-67.
[40] *Ibid.* 339.
[41] Philip, *Edinburgh to Salvador*, 45.

Willingen 1952 sought to rethink the nature of the missionary obligation of the church.[42] It was a significant milestone in the development of the theology of mission. During this conference, a new understanding of mission was created, which still acts as a compass and keeps Christians on track. This is why the conference is often spoken of as a "Copernican Revolution" in mission theology.[43] Since Willingen 1952, the term *Missio Dei* has been popularly used in contemporary mission studies, and it drew the course for a renewed, ecumenical understanding of mission. It was a pivotal date in a century marked by a profound change in the way people perceived the role of Christianity as one among other religions.[44] From Willingen onwards, a theocentric focus on mission as the *Missio Dei* replaced the former church-centric focus. Therefore, Christian mission is no longer seen as an assignment or obligation that the church sets itself, but rather, as the church originates from God's mission, mission becomes the essential quality of the church.[45]

Accra 1957-1958 emphasized two main issues: the significance of lay participation in mission and the creation of the Theological Education Fund (TEF; later renamed Programme for Theological Education).[46] The TEF aimed to aid the younger churches in studying theological issues of mission. Another significant issue at Accra 1957-58 was the constitutional provision for unifying with the World Council of Churches (WCC). New Delhi 1961 integrated the IMC and the WCC, wherein the former became the Division of World Mission and Evangelism.

Theology and Mission Methods of LIKBK vis-à-vis the IMC Process

The LIKBK moves in close proximity to the objectives of the IMC process. The mission statement of the LIKBK states that

> the basis of the Lairam Isua Krista Kohhran is the establishment of God's Kingdom on earth. The church was founded with the primary purpose that through its ministry, God's Kingdom will be inaugurated, made to grow and emerge with ever greater clarity. The Lairam Jesus Christ Baptist Church believes that God has called all the Lai people within and outside the boundaries of the Lai Autonomous District Council to be his people and serve him in unity.[47]

Furthermore, the LIKBK formulates the following objectives for mission work:

---

[42] Norman E. Thomas, ed., *Classic Texts in Mission & World Christianity* (Maryknoll, New York: Orbis Book, 1995), 103.
[43] Wilhelm Richebacher, "Missio Dei: The Basis of Mission Theology or A Wrong Path," in *International Review of Mission* 92:367 (Oct. 2003), 589.
[44] Wilhelm Richebacher, "Willingen 1952 – Willingen 2002 the Origin and Contents of This Edition of IRM" in *International Review of Mission* 92:367 (Oct. 2003), 463.
[45] Lothar Bauerochse, *Learning to Live Together: Interchurch Partnership as Ecumenical Communities of Learning* (Geneva: WCC Publication 2001), 42.
[46] Snaitang, *A History of Ecumenical Movement*, 112.
[47] *Constitution & Bye Laws of Lairam Jesus Christ Baptist Church*, 5.

a) Proclamation of the Gospel: The proclamation of the good news of the Kingdom of God in words and deeds – bringing people to Christ. The proclamation of the Gospel instructs the church and her mission workers to be agents of the evangelization of non-Christian lands and people.

b) Church Planting: To look after, consolidate and promote the present Lairam Jesus Christ Baptist Church and set up new churches wherever necessary.

c) Social Reform and Development: To safeguard basic human rights and freedom, to foster responsible concern for nature, to work for national and regional unity, to elevate social mindset and lifestyle, to work with Government and other organizations for the advancement of nation and society, encouraging responsible citizenship and the promotion of peace among all.

d) Aiding the Poor and Helpless: To assist and give aid to the poor, destitute widows, orphans, handicapped, social aliens and victims of natural calamities wherever possible, and working with organizations dedicated to these concerns.

e) Healing and Promoting Social Health: The church will tend to the sick, continuing the healing ministry of Jesus. It will set up and organize hospitals, clinics and health sub-centres wherever possible. It will also teach and stimulate social health and cleanliness and help in the formation of essential medical staff for this purpose.

f) Mission through literature and other means of communication: Publication of books and newspapers, organizing seminars and workshops for the propagation of essential Christian beliefs, setting up book rooms and printing press and the use of various means of communication in mission.

g) Mission in Education: Teaching and edifying members through Sunday school, Beirual lessons and various other methods. Promoting secular education by setting up important infrastructure.

h) Working with other Denominations and Welfare Groups: Establishing harmonious working relationships with other church denominations, Non-Governmental Organisations and Government social action groups for the good of the community.[48]

The IMC's conception of the inseparability of church and mission finds its praxis in the first mission objective of the LIKBK. It realizes Tambaram 1938's resolution about the church as the supreme agent of evangelization and the Willingen 1952 theme of the missionary obligation of the church. The objectives of the LIKBK reflect an ecumenical character of mission highlighting the continuity of ecumenism and concern for cooperation, a concern raised in Whitby 1947. Similarly, it took on matters of concern raised by the IMC, such as negotiations with governments, education, translation of the scriptures, production and distribution of Christian literature, securing religious liberties, efforts against the evils of narcotics, statistics and surveys, the establishment of schools, colleges and medical institutions and the training of missionaries.[49] The planting of churches as an objective reflects the IMC's emphasis on planting indigenous churches to establish younger churches, which the Council believed are the focal points of the plan and action previously mentioned.

---

[48] *Constitution & Bye Laws of Lairam Jesus Christ Baptist Church*, 2-4.
[49] Hogg, *Ecumenical Foundations*, 217.

Conclusion

In response to the question raised at the beginning of this paper about the connection between the IMC and the LIKBK, the following markers indicate certain common principles and objectives:

a. The spirit of ecumenism, cooperation and unity of church and mission,
b. Efforts at tackling the evil effects of narcotics,
c. The evangelization of non-Christian worlds,
d. Production of Christian literature,
e. School and medical institutions,
f. The social aspect of the Gospel,
g. Church Planting, and
h. Fight for victims of injustices

It must be noted that there are principles and objectives that the LIKBK shares with what was discussed in the IMC process. The ecumenical concern raised in the formation and functioning of the IMC in its meetings at Lake Mohonk, Jerusalem, Tambaram, Whitby and Willingen has embedded features that are visible in the mission theology and motives of the LIKBK, an ecumenical ecclesial body, formed in the midst of a Christian world haphazardly dominated and influenced by detrimental denominationalism.

Relationship of Churches in the Mission Fields in Northeast India: Prospects and Challenges

Lalfakawma Ralte

Eight subjects were selected as the key themes for discussion at the World Missionary Conference at Edinburgh in 1910. One of these themes was "the Church in the Mission Field,"[1] which considered missionary problems in countries where Christ had never been proclaimed. The discussions at Edinburgh in 1910 and the subsequent years in the International Missionary Council (IMC) process have generated discussions on missionary relations with culture, mission theology and cooperation in mission. This contribution examines how these discussions continue to shape Christian missions in various parts of the world, particularly in Mizoram, Northeast India. It delves into the relationship between two Mizo churches, the Presbyterian Church of India, Mizoram Synod and the Baptist Church of Mizoram (BCM), in their mission fields in Arunachal Pradesh, another state in Northeast India.

For decades, different mission agencies have been operating in Arunachal Pradesh, also known as the "Land of the Rising Sun." On the one hand, their presence has aided the numerical growth of Christianity. On the other hand, it is a cause of friction between missionaries and native Christian converts. Amidst the array of common irritations, two issues stand out: sheep-stealing and denominational conflicts. This situation bears an uncanny resemblance to the historical context that initiated discussions on mission cooperation and unity in the nineteenth century, paving the way for the modern ecumenical movement. What might MPC and BCM missions and mission churches in Arunachal Pradesh learn from past missionary cooperation? This contribution appraises the relationship between the two missionary-sending churches and explores the prospects for future cooperation.

The Religious Beliefs of the People of Arunachal Pradesh

According to the 2011 census, 30.26 percent of Arunachal Pradesh's total population of 13.84 lakhs are Christians. Thus Christians are the largest religious group in the state and Christianity is the majority religion in four of Arunachal Pradesh's sixteen districts.[2] Hindus account for 29.04 per cent of the total population. Buddhists comprise 11.77 per cent of the population. Muslims

---

[1] Kenneth Scott Latourette, "Ecumenical Bearings of the Missionary Movement and the International Missionary Council," in *A History of the Ecumenical Movement 1517-1948*, eds. Ruth Rouse and Stephen Charles Neil (London: SPCK,1954), 355-356.
[2] "List of districts in Arunachal Pradesh, 2023", accessed January 12, 2023, https://www.findeasy.in/list-of-districts-in-arunachal-pradesh.

constitute 1.95 per cent of the population. The followers of *Dony Polo*[3] and those who do not identify with any religion account for 26.20 per cent[4] of the people.

The Origin and Development of Missionary Work in Arunachal Pradesh

Two British commissioners of Assam, David Scott and Francis Jenkins, made the first known attempts to evangelize the people of Arunachal Pradesh soon after signing the Treaty of Yandaboo[5] in 1826. At the request of Scott, the British Missionary Society (BMS) opened the first mission station in Guwahati, Assam,[6] in 1829, which paved the way for Christian mission to reach out to both peoples of the plains and hills in and around Assam. James Rae was the first full-time missionary of the BMS in Assam. The BMS started a small school in Guwahati, which was then the centre of the whole Northeast region of British India. Rae worked under the close supervision of Scott,[7] whose enthusiasm for the proclamation of the Gospel was unprecedented. Francis Jenkins, Chief Commissioner of Assam, requested the American Baptists to send another missionary to Assam. As a result, the American Baptists sent two missionaries to Sadiya. They were Nathan and Eliza Brown, who arrived at Sadiya on March 23, 1836.[8]

In 1839, the initial Christian mission work in Arunachal Pradesh was undertaken by the American Baptist missionary Miles Bronson, who briefly resided in Namsanghea village, marking the inaugural missionary endeavour in the region.[9] The next contact came through Catholic missionary fathers Nicholas Michael Krick and Augustine-Etienne Bourry, who entered present-day Arunachal Pradesh inhabited by Adi and Mishmi on the way to Tibet in 1853.[10] Another effort towards Christian mission work in Arunachal was made by J.H. Lorrain and F.W. Savidge, who founded the Assam Frontier Mission in London and sailed for India towards the end of 1899. In June 1900, they arrived and settled in Sadiya and thereafter began working among the Adi, Mishing, and

---

[3] *Donyi Polo* is the religion of the indigenous people of Arunachal Pradesh in which worshipping the sun and moon is the key element.
[4] "Arunachal Pradesh Religion Census 2011", accessed October 10, 2021, http://www.census2011.co.in/data/religion/state/12-arunachal-pradesh/html.
[5] The Treaty of Yandaboo, signed on February 24, 1826, marked the end of the First Anglo-Burmese War, which had been raging for two years. The treaty was signed between the East India Company and the King of Ava, with the former emerging as the victor. See "Treaty of Yandaboo", accessed January 11, 2023, www.gktoday.in/topic/treaty-of-yandabu/.
[6] Frederick S. Downs, *History of Christianity in India*, Volume V, Part 5 (Bangalore: CHAI, 2003), 33, 37.
[7] The letter of J. Marshman, July 9, 1829, PASM, No, IV, 1829, 238.
[8] Jumto Ngomdir, *Arunachal Presbyterian Church: Presbyterian Church of India*, 2nd ed. (Itanagar: Arunachal and Assam Mission Field West, 2013), 1.
[9] "Letter of Mr. Bronson, January 6, 1841" *BMM, Vol. XXI, No. 10* (October 1841), 295.
[10] Lalfakawma Ralte, *Ni Leh Thla Betute Zinga Pathian Hnathawh Ropui* (Wondrous Works of God in Arunachal Pradesh) (Aizawl: Lalchamliana Tlau, 2012), 48.

Mishmi. They applied to the British government in Sadiya to enter the hills, and to their great surprise, were granted permission to do so almost immediately. They developed for the Adi language a system of writing suitable for the use of the indigenous people and compiled *A Dictionary of the Abor-Miri Language* in 1910.[11] Among the missionaries who also came to the front were N.E. Grass, P.O. Williams, John Firth, L.W.B. Jackman, John Selender and Jackman.

In contrast to other areas in Northeast India which saw the introduction and growth of Christianity in the nineteenth and early twentieth centuries, Christianity neither took firm root nor won the hearts of the people of Arunachal during the colonial era.[12] However, despite many missionary activities in the state, as Nani Bath observes, "there was not a single recorded Christian in Arunachal Pradesh in [the] 1951" Indian Census.[13]

In the case of Arunachal Pradesh, Western missionaries can be called the torchbearers of the Gospel since they were the ones who initiated the works of the Gospel in the region. Yet, the actual people who should be credited for the transformation of the lives of the indigenous people in Arunachal Pradesh are the missionaries from Mizoram and Nagaland.[14]

Start of Mission Fields in Arunachal Pradesh by MPC and BCM

The Christian mission work of the MPC and BCM in Arunachal Pradesh began as a ministry of help at the request of existing churches in the region. The MPC began mission work in Arunachal Pradesh at the request of the Upper Siang Baptist Christian Association (USBCA) to take it as its mission field. Subsequently, the two parties cooperated in mission through an agreement that recognised the USBCA as a mission field of the MPC with effect from June 1, 1984.[15] The MPC opened three mission fields in the region following the agreement. The first was opened at Lakla, in the eastern part of the state, on January 27, 1991.[16] Rev. K. Lalthangmawia was the first Field Secretary of the Arunachal Mission Field. He was inducted by Rev. K. Lalzuala, the then Moderator of the Presbyterian Church of India, Mizoram Synod.[17] It was followed by the opening of another mission field at Itanagar, the state capital, on April 1, 2001.[18] The opening of the new Mission Field and the induction of the

---

[11] Lalfakawma Ralte, *Ni Leh Thla,* 50.
[12] See Ralte, Lalfakawma. "Impact of Christianity among Adi Tribe of Arunachal Pradesh" (Master of Theology diss., Senate of Serampore College University, 2014).
[13] Nani Bath, "Understanding Religious Policy of Arunachal Pradesh", accessed September 24, 2021, http://www.asthabharati.org/Dia_Jan06?Nani.htm.
[14] Cf. Ralte, "Impact of Christianity among Adi Tribe of Arunachal Pradesh," 59.
[15] R. Lalchangliana, "Reports of Arunachal and Assam Mission Field West," in *Silver Jubilee Celebration, Arunachal Presbyterian Church*, ed. Lalfakawma Ralte (Boleng: Field Working Committee, AAMFW, 2009), 1-5.
[16] Lalfakawma Ralte, *Ni Leh Thla* , 68.
[17] *Ibid.*
[18] Interview with Rev. R. Vanlalnghaka (Pastor in-charge Chanmari Pastorate, Aizawl), September 25, 2021. He served as the Field Secretary of the Arunachal and Assam Mission Field West during 2001-2003.

Field Secretary were done at the Chapel of St. Peter's English Medium School. Rev. C. Rosiama, the then Executive Secretary, in charge of Mission, inducted Rev. R. Valalnghaka as Field Secretary of Arunachal and Assam Field West.[19] The Arunachal and Assam Mission Field West were registered with the Government of Arunachal Pradesh under the Society Registration Act 1860 bearing no. SR/ITA/1006. The office of the Field was shifted from St. Peter's School to Itanagar on March 1, 2002.[20] The third mission field, Arunachal and Assam Mission Field North was inaugurated at Aalo, the northern part of the state, on March 11, 2016.[21] In 2020, the MPC mission headquarters in Arunachal Pradesh was relocated to Pasighat for geographical convenience. This field comprises of five districts of Arunachal Pradesh, viz., Siang, East Siang, West Siang, Upper Subansari, Shy Yomi and one district of Assam, that is, Demaji.[22] There are six pastorates under this Mission Field at Aalo, Boleng, Daporijo, Tato, Pasighat and Jonai.

The initiation of the BCM mission in Arunachal Pradesh followed a similar pattern to that of the MPC mission. The BCM began operating in Arunachal Pradesh in 1990 at the Adi Baptist Union's (ABU) request.[23] The ABU was formed on February 1, 1971.[24] The BCM did not plant or form churches of its own. Rather, it works where the ABU had already planted churches.

The Influence of the Formation of the IMC on the Theology of Mission Agencies

The discussions in the IMCs highlighted the social dimension of the Gospel and the importance of Christian engagement in society. One of the functions of the first meeting of the IMC in October 1921 at Lake Mohonk was "to help unite Christian public opinion in support of freedom of conscience and religion and missionary liberty."[25] In the same vein, pastors and missionaries working under the MPC and BCM have encouraged indigenous church workers and leaders in Arunachal Pradesh[26] to initiate forums to discuss social issues. Consequently, in big towns, Christians from different denominations have come together and formed Christian forums. Most of these forums focus on defending the Christian faith against external threats such as *Hindutva*.[27]

---

[19] Vanlalnghaka, interview.
[20] Vanlalnghaka, interview.
[21] Interview with Rev. Lalhmuchhuaka (Field Secretary, Arunachal and Assam Mission Field North, Pasighat), October 1, 2021.
[22] *Arunachal Vartian – Arunachal and Assam Mission Field North* (Pasighat: AAMFN, FWC, 2021), 14.
[23] Interview with Vanlalchhunga (missionary working in Adi and Galo areas, Arunachal Pradesh), September 24, 2021.
[24] "The Adi Baptist Union", accessed February 2, 2023, https://www.adibaptistunion.org.
[25] See Latourette, "Ecumenical Bearings," 367.
[26] Interview with C. Lalramdina (missionary who is working in AAMFW, Arunachal Pradesh), October 1, 2021.
[27] Hindutva is popularly translated as Hindu-ness and a good many Hindus simply think of it as the idea and practice of living a life according to Hindu teachings.

One of the three outstanding issues discussed in the second conference of the IMC on Mount of Olives, Jerusalem, 1928, was the issue of the social dimension of the Gospel.[28] After missionary work began in Arunachal Pradesh, both the MPC and BCM gave attention to this aspect by opening schools and dispensaries. The MPC regularly sends evangelist-teachers to the various schools it has established in the state. It also deploys missionary nurses and doctors to spread health education and give medical help.

The BCM has also conducted medical camps and the like in collaboration with the Government of Arunachal Pradesh in different villages. Church members also occasionally organize blood donation camps, voluntarily donating their blood.

Socio-cultural Changes as a Result of the Church's Missions

Christian mission played an important role in bringing about socio-cultural changes in Arunachal Pradesh. Traditionally, Arunachali society was divided into free people, freed slaves and actual slaves.[29] Almost all the tribes of Arunachal used to raid the plains of the Brahmaputra valley and carry away slaves to their hills.[30] Slave trade existed between the Adi and Mishing people in Arunachal Pradesh throughout the British colonial period, from 1826 to 1947. As a result of concerted efforts made by missionaries in Northeast India, particularly Peter Fraser, who worked in Mizoram, and missionaries under the American Baptist mission such as Nathan Brown, who worked in Assam, the British Government reluctantly prohibited the slavery system in Northeast India,[31] including in Arunachal Pradesh.

Despite the British government's abolition of slavery in Arunachal Pradesh, the harsh reality persisted, with many people still being held in bondage. Fraser was a tireless advocate for the abolition of slavery in the British-occupied territories of Northeast India. In correspondence with the British Indian government, he pleaded with them to end slavery as quickly as possible.[32] The British Government was forced to order the release slaves in northeast India, including those in Arunachal Pradesh, due to persistent pressure from missionaries. The local churches and missionaries from Mizoram continued to

---

[28] B.M. Thomas, *Edinburgh 1910 and the International Missionary Council (IMC), with Special Reference to the IMC as Means of Involving Asian and African Christians in Ecumenical Movement up till 1961* (Federated Faculty for Research in Religion and Culture, Kottayam, July 28, 2015). *Cf.* "Edinburgh 1910 and the IMC", accessed February 10, 2023,
https://www.academia.edu/19351072/Edinburgh_1910_and_the_IMC.
[29] P. Thankappan Nair, *Tribes of Arunachal Pradesh* (Guwahati: Spectrum Publications, 1985), 151.
[30] D. Pandey, *History of Arunachal Pradesh: Early Times to 1972 AD* (Pasighat: Bani Mandir Publishing House, 1997), 64- 65.
[31] Downs, *History of Christianity in India,* 150- 151.
[32] Lal Dena, *Christian Missionaries and Colonialism – a Study of Movement in Northeast India with Particular Reference to Manipur and Lushai Hills 1894-1947* (Shillong: Vendrame Institute, 1988), 76.

cooperate in fighting against slavery in Arunachal Pradesh and finally, in 1960, it was abolished in the entire state.[33] This was a period when all foreign missionaries had already been expelled from independent India.

Before British colonial rule and the arrival of missionaries, Arunachal Pradesh experienced frequent inter-tribal and inter-village conflicts. However, with the advent of British colonial rule and the influence of Christian missionaries, these hostilities significantly diminished, particularly in areas where Christianity was prevalent. According to Zomuansanga, this protracted problem among the various tribes of Arunachal Pradesh was solved, "at least among Christian members who flow together as one despite their differences in terms of tribes and ethnicities. That is because Christianity teaches them to love one another."[34] Despite the cessation of inter-tribe warfare, a contemporary challenge lingers as the various tribes continue to grapple with harmonious coexistence. This challenge can be traced back to the communal animosity that originated in the pre-Christian era.

Missionaries introduced new roles within the community, including pastors, missionaries, evangelists, teachers, and other positions associated with the church and the propagation of the Kingdom of God. These roles primarily benefited Christian leaders. Regrettably, the creation of these white-collar jobs led to a division among the people, separating those with wages from those without. As a result, mission agencies inadvertently contributed to economic stratification and social division.

Challenges

While there are numerous positive aspects to the missions of the MPC and BCM, they also grapple with practical challenges, including denominational conflicts and disputes arising from competition and issues such as sheep-stealing. A study conducted through questionnaires sent to missionaries working under the MPC and BCM in the Arunachal mission field shows the following results:

Sl. No.	Do you agree that the MPC and BCM operate harmoniously in the Arunachal field?	Respondents	Percentage
1.	Strongly Agree	0	0
2.	Agree	2	6.6
3.	Undecided	6	20
4.	Disagree	18	60
5.	Strongly Disagree	4	13.4
	Total	**30**	**100**

Observing the data, it's evident that the MPC and BCM missions in Arunachal Pradesh lack harmonious collaboration. Why does this lack of mutual cooperation exist? One contributing factor is the strong emphasis placed by both

---

[33] Lalfakawma Ralte, *Ni leh Thla*, 46.
[34] Interview with Zomuansanga Chhangte (Pastor in-charge of Boleng Pastorate, 2012-2016), September 16, 2021.

BCM and MPC leaders on numbers and figures. The sending churches prioritize congregational growth and the increase in new believers, pressuring their missionaries to deliver reports of growing numbers. This approach leads to two notable consequences: firstly, it fosters competition and potential sheep-stealing, and secondly, it places a greater focus on quantity over quality in missionary work.

Why is the cooperation that characterised the early mission work not evident now? Missionaries from the BMS and Arthington Mission were foreigners, few in number who kept to their designated areas and did not get involved or interfere with each other's work. A shift can be seen when mission bodies stopped sending foreign missionaries and the Indian churches began sending Indian missionaries. Rather than collaborating with fellow Indian missionaries, they encountered friction and conflicts when working in the same mission field, highlighting a prevalent sense of competition over cooperation in mission work.

Contrary to the prior assumption that Presbyterian and Baptist churches in Mizoram are known for mission cooperation, the situation in Arunachal Pradesh proved to be the opposite. In the 1980s, an imaginary boundary was established to delineate the areas of operation for MPC and BCM missionaries, aiming to reduce potential friction. Nevertheless, rumours of missionaries from both missions crossing this imaginary boundary triggered tension and friction among those working in the region.[35] The differences between the denominations become points for disagreements and hindered cooperation. Different baptism practices became a source of disagreement among missionaries and believers. The BCM advocated for full immersion in water, while the MPC favoured sprinkling water on the believer's head. These conflicting views on valid baptism not only caused friction but also gave rise to unwanted rivalry between BCM and MPC missionaries. Furthermore, they weakened Christian unity by emphasizing denominational doctrinal differences.

The unhealthy competition between the two mission-sending bodies can be attributed to several factors. First, there is a lack of awareness of ecumenism among some missionaries of both MPC and BCM, and this can be attributed in part to inadequate training provided by their sending bodies. Secondly, insufficient cooperation and coordination among the leaders of MPC and BCM contribute to this undesirable competition in the mission field. The absence of encouragement for an ecumenical spirit and instances of perceived supremacy among some leaders discourage missionaries from fostering unity. Furthermore, the ecumenical movement faces challenges due to a lack of direction and harmonization among its diverse participants. It is essential to address pressing challenges and focus on strengthening denominational fellowships rather than merely expanding ecumenism.

Conclusion

The study of cooperation in mission in Arunachal Pradesh shows a strange ambivalence. While Western missionaries first brought the Gospel to the hills of

---

[35] Lalramdina, interview

Arunachal Pradesh and cooperated amongst themselves to some extent in mission work on the ground, the indigenous people of Arunachal did not readily accept their message. The resistance of the local people to anything foreign might be a reason for the slow growth of Christianity during the colonial period. Only after Mizos and Nagas sent by churches in Northeast India began preaching the Gospel among them did Christianity begin to grow in Arunachal Pradesh. Christians have now become the largest religious group in the state. The increasingly positive attitude towards native culture, the development of holistic mission theology and the realization of the need for cooperation in mission are legacies of the IMC process that have influenced churches and missions in the region. However, despite the growth of Christianity, missionaries from various denominations and missionary-sending bodies from the Northeast to Arunachal Pradesh find it hard to cooperate harmoniously with each other. An analysis of mission practices in Arunachal Pradesh by both the MPC and BCM reveals a mixture of progress and challenges in terms of cooperative mission efforts. The pressure to expand Christian membership has driven growth but has also given rise to conflicts among various Christian groups. During the presence of foreign missionaries in Arunachal Pradesh, there was a stronger emphasis on unity and cooperation transcending denominational boundaries. However, in later periods, indigenous church missionaries became more focused on the growth of their specific church and denomination, which diminished the spirit of ecumenism and church unity.

This paper contends that a study of the spirit of Edinburgh 1910 and the IMC can enhance awareness of ecumenism, offering improved education about ecumenism for missionaries and rekindling a call for cooperation and unity between BMC and MPC. This call underscores the importance of working harmoniously and fostering mutual understanding.

III. Mission Theology and Theological Formation

From *Ad Gentes* to New Evangelization: Roman Catholic Missionary Trajectories

Francis Thonippara

This contribution aims to outline the Roman Catholic Church's missionary efforts in the 20th and 21st centuries and mainly presents the papal teachings and the teachings of the Second Vatican Council. The twentieth century has rightly been called "the century of missions." The spread of the Church in Asia and Africa, the birth of indigenous churches and native leadership and the active involvement of foreign and local missionaries, and the branching off of many religious congregations in the Asian and African soil testify to the missionary vitality of the Church. Although the two world wars adversely affected mission work, the timely papal interventions and the radical commitment of the missionaries were able to overcome the threats posed by the two wars. A series of papal encyclicals, exhortations and letters gave further vitality and new directions to the mission commitment.

We see a reawakening of the missionary consciousness among the Protestant churches from the very beginning of the twentieth century. The Edinburgh Missionary Conference of 1910, the International Missionary Council (IMC) of 1921, and a chain of international missionary conferences at Jerusalem in 1928, Tambaram in 1938, Whitby in 1947, Willingen in 1952, Ghana in 1957 and others speak loudly about the interests of various churches in mission work, and that too in the changing contexts of new challenges.

Papal Interventions

Pope Benedict XV's (1914-1922) Apostolic Letter *Maximum Illud* (that Momentous), dated November 30, 1919, gave a new impetus to the missionary task of proclaiming the Gospel. The document stressed the importance of indigenous clergy, inculturation, local churches and theology of mission and reminded the Catholics of their part in mission work. The Pope sharply rejected all European nationalistic tendencies in the mission field.[1] On the occasion of the centenary of *Maximum Illud,* Pope Francis (2013-) declared October 2019 an extraordinary mission month and expressed the wish that the centenary would be an occasion to open ourselves to the joyful newness of the Gospel.

Pope Pius XI (1922-1939) regarded the oversight of missions as the primary duty of the papacy and energetically took charge of advancing the propagation of the faith. An international Catholic Missions Congress was held in 1922 to celebrate the three-hundredth anniversary of the Congregation of the

---

[1] Bihlmeyer-Tuechle, *Church History, Modern and Recent Times*, Vol. III (Paderborn: Ferdinand Schoeningh, 1966), 531.

Propagation of the Faith. In 1925, a great Missions Exhibit was organized at the Vatican. Importantly, on February 28, 1926, the Pope issued his great mission encyclical *Rerum Ecclesiae* (Things of the Church). He appealed to missionaries to devote themselves more strongly to the Church's intimate relationship with the mission countries and the assimilation of the Church into the local culture. He pushed not only for the training of native priests and catechists but also for the establishment of communities of male and female religious.[2] The document stresses the founding, solidification and independence of the newly established church communities. In 1927, a permanent Missions Museum was founded at the Lateran in Rome; and in 1932, a Missiological Institute was inaugurated at the Propaganda College in Rome, and a faculty of Missiology with several professorships was established at the Gregorian University in the same city.

The Pope exhorted bishops in their home regions to offer their enthusiastic collaboration and support. He also stressed the importance of mission superiors creating larger groups of native priests and bishops, along with the establishment of regional seminaries for the training of future native clergy. During the reign of Pius XI (1922-1939), almost two hundred mission dioceses were established, of which forty, for the first time, were entrusted to native bishops. In the twentieth century, India was the first to have the honour of seeing an Indian receiving an episcopal office in the Latin Church. This was a Jesuit, Francis T. Roche, who was appointed bishop of Tuticorin when it was made a diocese and handed over to the Indian secular clergy on June 12, 1923.[3] The Catholic Thomas Christians had native bishops as far back as in 1663 and 1782, and from 1896 onwards, they had native bishops without a break. The Indian Jacobite Church had native bishops from 1653.

Pope Pius XII (1939-1958) established the College of St. Peter on June 29, 1948. This institution was designed for priests of missionary background to pursue advanced studies in Rome.[4] The encyclicals of Pius XII, *Evangelii Praecones* (Preaching of the Gospel) on June 11, 1951, and *Fidei Donum* (Gift of Faith) on April 21, 1957, show his eagerness to expedite the establishment of indigenous churches with their own bishops and his recognition of the increasing role that the laity played in this regard. He also took a more positive attitude towards the ecumenical movement.[5] The first encyclical emphasizes the importance of education, especially at a time when Communism was spreading rapidly. The encyclical of Pope John XXIII (1958-1963), *Princeps Pastorum* (Prince of the Shepherds), published on November 28, 1959, stresses the importance of missionary undertakings, native clergy and lay participation in mission engagement.

Together with the salvation of souls (*salus animarum*), missionaries were duty-bound to fight against injustices and to work towards the development of

---

[2] Hubert Jedin (ed.), *History of the Church, The Church in the Modern World*, Vol. X (London: Burns & Oates, 1981), 359.
[3] Roger Aubert (ed.), *The Christian Centuries: The Church in Secularised Society*, Vol. V (NY: Paulist Press, 1978), 403.
[4] Aubert, *The Christian Centuries*, 400.
[5] *Ibid.* 568.

an egalitarian society. This was closely bound with the Roman Catholic Church's concern for maintaining and strengthening solidarity between the rich and the deprived nations throughout the process of decolonization. Political independence did not appear to her an absolute good. She wanted to be sure that the acquisition of political independence did not impair the collaboration between nations on which the development of all peoples depended. This preoccupation was given clear expression in the encyclicals *Mater et Magistra* (Mother and Teacher), dated May 15, 1961, and *Pacem in Terris* (Peace on Earth), dated April 11, 1963, published by Pope John XXIII and in the encyclical *Populorum Progressio* (Progress of the Nations) of March 26, 1967 from his successor, Pope Paul VI (1963-1978), which was devoted exclusively to the developing countries.[6] These encyclicals indicated the Roman Catholic Church's concern for the holistic upliftment and development of the people of God, and added a new dimension to mission work. However, it may be argued that the influence of liberation theology and new understanding and approaches to other religions in the light of the teachings of the Second Vatican Council, diluted, to a great extent, the missionary spirit and enthusiasm of the Roman Catholic Church.

Second Vatican Council (1962-1965) and Further Developments

The Second Vatican Council was a watershed moment in the history of the Roman Catholic Church, which widened her horizons. Pope John XXIII convened the Council with the intention of infusing new life into the Church by metaphorically opening the windows and bringing about the much-needed *aggiornamento* or renewal. The Council was an attempt on the part of the Church to enter into dialogue with the modern world. Dialogue was the keyword of the Council- dialogue with the world, with the churches and dialogue with other religions. The Council produced sixteen documents, four constitutions, nine decrees and three declarations.

Ad Gentes (To the Nations) is the Second Vatican Council's Decree on missionary activity. It announces the Roman Catholic Church's commitment to bringing the Gospel to all people. This Decree reminds the Catholic faithful about their fundamental duty and obligation of preaching the Word of God and reaffirms the close link between evangelization and the upliftment of the marginalized or the holistic growth of the poor and the less privileged in society. Thus, we observe a notable change in the tone of the Decree where evangelization means not only preaching the Gospel but also caring for the welfare of the people. Ad Gentes also emphasizes the formation of robust Christian communities and fostering harmonious relations with other Christian churches, underscoring the importance of ecumenism and discouraging the rivalry between different church denominations that was prevalent during the early phase of church missionary endeavours The document also stresses the importance of training future missionaries to meet the challenges of the modern world. This document was promulgated on December 7, 1965, by Pope Paul VI.

---

[6] *Ibid.* 426.

This Council emphasizes the urgency of mission work and asserts that every member of the body of Christ has an obligation to help the body grow. To encourage mission work, several documents have been published in the course of time. *Evangelii Nuntiandi* (Preaching of the Gospel) is an apostolic exhortation issued on December 8, 1975, by Pope Paul VI following the work of the Synod on the theme in 1974. It deals with evangelism and affirms the role of every Christian in spreading the Catholic religion. *Evangelii Nuntiandi* tells us how to evangelize or proclaim the message of the Gospel in the context of the present situation. If we want to evangelize, we must proclaim the Gospel and to proclaim the Gospel is also by life witnessing (Number 2). The formation of ecclesiastical communities is recommended for effective mission.

Nostra Aetate (In our Times), the Second Vatican Council's Declaration on the Relation of the Church to non-Christian Religions, was published on October 28, 1965. The declaration calls for Roman Catholics to recognize the value of non-Christian religions and the fellowship among followers of different faiths. "The Catholic Church rejects nothing which is true and holy in these religions" (Number 2). The declaration concludes with an emphatic rejection of discrimination based on religion, race, colour or condition of life, and it calls for universal respect for human dignity and human rights (Number 5).

The Indian Scenario

The Roman Catholic Church in India considered how to implement the teachings of the Second Vatican Council by organizing the "All India Seminar on Church in India Today" in Bangalore in 1969. This Seminar echoed the need for radical social change that would afford justice for the poor and the underprivileged. This would require the existing social order be radically reformed so that the fruits of development may be equally shared.[7] Another major event was "The International Theological Conference on Evangelization and Dialogue" at Nagpur in 1971. The declaration of this Theological Conference was articulated in 53 articles which was a comprehensive understanding of the new way of being a Christian in India. Articles 30 to 37 speak about liberation and development and stress that development must be integral and human (Nos. 30-37). The very title of the edited volume *Service and Salvation* sheds light on the new shift in proclaiming the Word of God through the holistic growth of the people.[8] This major event was soon followed by the "National Consultation on Evangelization" at Patna in October 1973. This National Consultation called for a prophetic Church which could identify with the poor. The cry of this consultation was "fully Indian and authentically Christian." Thus, in light of the teachings of the Second Vatican Council, the Roman Catholic Church in India initiated a process of rethinking and revitalizing its mission. She has been engaged in a search, a discernment of the ways or paths of mission in the

---

[7] See *All-India Seminar on Church in India Today, Bangalore, 1969* (New Delhi: CBCI Centre, 1970), 244-245.
[8] See Joseph Pathrapankal, CMI (ed.), *Service and Salvation* (Bangalore: Theological Publications in India, 1973), 1-16.

historical context of the lives of the Catholics. There is a growing conviction that the context determines the path of the mission. This search is a sign of the growing maturity of the Church and its determination to become a truly local Church. Augustine Kanjamala captures this conviction when he states that "participation in the struggles of the people for full human dignity and involvement in actions for justice have been found to be valid forms of mission. The involvement of the laity in such ventures is a sign of the vitality of the Church's mission."[9]

In the face of the changes in mission theology, the Roman Catholic Church in India took seriously the issues related to Dalits, Tribals and women. The General Body Meeting of the Catholic Bishops Conference of India (CBCI) held in Pune in 1992 dealt with these specific issues. Another focus was on the evolution of local churches and the evangelization of cultures. The Church's mission to transform the world through the values of the Gospel should be in tune with the spirit of reverence for nature embedded in the culture, spirituality and lifestyle of India. In this context, the Church itself should manifest a deep reverence for the earth and courageously exploit the fallacy of those who, for selfish interests, exploit nature at the expense of the harmony of the cosmos and to the detriment of others. It is part of the evangelizing mission of the Church to promote a greater sense of harmony and balance, a spirit of partnership with nature, an attitude of stewardship and to denounce the mentality of profit-oriented domination and exploitation of the earth that surrounds our life.[10]

New Evangelization

The legacy of *Lumen Gentium* (The Light of the Nations), one of the foundational texts of the modern Roman Catholic Church, *Ad Gentes* and later documents have been the Church's initiative for New Evangelization in the Third Millennium. New Evangelization is the particular process by which baptized members of the Catholic Church express the general Christian call to evangelization. There has been a special focus on Europe and the Americas, areas that have traditionally been Roman Catholic, but which have been heavily influenced by secularization. The stress is also on re-evangelizing Christians who have fallen away from the faith.

The first papal use of the term "New Evangelization" was by Pope Paul VI in his 1975 Apostolic Exhortation *Evangelii Nuntiandi*. Other papal documents on New Evangelization include *Redemptoris Missio* (The Mission of the Redeemer), 1990, *Tertio Millennio adveniente* (As the Third Millennium Approaches), 1994, *Novo Millennio ineunte* (At the beginning of the new Millennium), 2001, *Ecclesia in Europa* (The Church in Europe), 2003, *Ubicumque et Semper* (Everywhere and Always), 2010, *Lineamenta* (In general, a text written in preparation for a General Assembly of the Synod of Bishops on

---

[9] Augustine Kanjamala, SVD (ed.), *Paths of Mission in India Today* (Bombay: St Pauls, 1996), 251. This is a portion taken from the background paper for the Pune Consultation in 1994.
[10] *Ibid.* 260. A portion of the background paper for the Pune Consultation in 1994.

New Evangelization), 2011 and *Evangelii Gaudium* (The Joy of the Gospel), 2013. Evangelization of presence is very much stressed in *Evangelii Nuntiandi* numbers 22 and 41. New Evangelization is also becoming necessary because of the large number of immigrations all over the world. *Redemptoris Missio* states,

> Everywhere, then, a renewed proclamation is needed even for those already baptized. Many Europeans today think they know what Christianity is, yet they do not really know it at all. Often they are lacking in knowledge of the most basic elements and notions of the faith. Many of the baptized live as if Christ did not exist; The challenge frequently consists not so much in baptizing new converts as in enabling those already baptized to be converted to Christ and His Gospel. In our communities we need to be seriously concerned about bringing the Gospel of hope to all those who are far from the faith or have abandoned the practice of Christianity (R.M. number 47).

Again, we read in *Redemptoris Missio* number 3, "I sense that the moment has come to commit all of the Church's energies to a new evangelization and to the mission *ad gentes*. No believer in Christ, no institution of the Church, can avoid this supreme duty: to proclaim Christ to all peoples." *Redemptoris Missio* (The Mission of the Redeemer), subtitled, "On the permanent validity of the Church's missionary mandate," is a papal encyclical by Pope John Paul II published on December 7, 1990, devoted to the subject of the urgency of the missionary activity and in which he wishes to invite the Church to renew her missionary commitment. *Redemptoris Missio* is a *magna carta* of New Evangelization: "Without doubt a mending of the Christian fabric of society is urgently needed in all parts of the world. But for this to come about what is needed is to first remake the Christian fabric of the ecclesial community itself present in these countries and nations". (RM number 34).

With *Ubicumque et Semper* in 2010, Pope Benedict XVI (2005-2013) established the Pontifical Council for Promoting the New Evangelization. According to the *Lineamenta* mentioned above, New Evangelization is:

> the courage to forge new paths in responding to the changing circumstances and conditions facing the Church in her call to proclaim and live the Gospel today. The New Evangelization is primarily a spiritual activity capable of recapturing in our times the courage and forcefulness of the first Christians and the first missionaries. Consequently, it requires, first of all, a process of discerning the vitality of Christianity and a reconsideration of its accomplishments and the difficulties it has encountered (Lineamenta, number 5).

The goal of evangelization is the transmission of the Christian faith. New methods and new forms of expression are needed to convey to the people of today the perennial truth of Jesus Christ. This renewed dynamism in the Christian community will lead to renewed missionary activity, now more urgent than ever.

In 2013, Pope Francis published *Evangelii Gaudium,* an Apostolic Exhortation, which is the document of the XIII General Assembly of the Synod of Bishops gathered from October 7-28, 2012, to discuss the theme "The New Evangelization for the Transmission of the Christian Faith". By this exhortation, the Pope challenges the faithful to live in accordance with the missionary command. In *Evangelii Gaudium* the Pope wishes to encourage the Christian faithful to embark upon a new chapter of evangelization marked by joy while pointing out new paths for the Church's journey in the years to come. The New Evangelization is a summons addressed to all, and is carried out in three principal settings: (i) Ordinary pastoral ministry (to inflame the hearts of the faithful); (ii) Outreach to the baptized whose lives do not reflect the demands of baptism; and (iii) Evangelization of those who do not know Jesus Christ or who have always rejected him.[11] In number 27, we read: "I dream of a missionary option, that is, a missionary impulse capable of transforming everything, so that the Church's customs, ways of doing things, times and schedules, language and structures can be suitably channelled for the evangelization of today's world rather than for her self-preservation." Pope Francis calls for our Church to thrive by choosing the missionary option in everything that we do. To show the true face of the Church, 2015 was declared the "Year of Mercy". The Church has always had a mandate for missions and evangelism, and this accompanies the Church into the new Third Millennium (*Novo Millennio ineunte*, number 58).

Fratelli Tutti (All Brothers), the latest encyclical of Pope Francis, published on October 4, 2020, aims at the realization of the prayer we make in 'Our Father' where we pray that all are brothers and sisters because we are children of one Father. For Pope Francis, fraternity is the phrase proper to the Kingdom of God, in which the Holy Spirit can come, dwell and act. He wants to remind the whole of humanity through this encyclical that the values of the Kingdom of God transcend all barriers, and the meaning of the Kingdom of God is the ability of Christians to make the Good News of the Gospel available to all humanity, to all men and women without distinction, as a resource of salvation and fullness. This Gospel fraternity makes the Christian religion more relevant in the post-modern world and thus the new form of evangelization. Pope Francis insists throughout his papacy that the Christian faith is even today relevant, provided the Christians live the authentic Christian faith, the evangelization of presence. Pope Francis might have been influenced by St. Theresa of Kolkata, who practiced the inner spirit of *Fratelli Tutti,* and thus became a living saint for the whole of humanity, a mother to all, including her own Hindu and Muslim brothers and sisters.

To revitalize the mission commitment of the Church, Pope Francis restructured the Roman Curia, the central administration of the Roman Catholic Church. After many years of hard work and teamwork, he published the Apostolic Constitution *Praedicate Evangelium* (Preach the Gospel)[12] on March 19, 2022, which came into effect in June 2022. This Apostolic Constitution replaces the *Pastor Bonus* of Pope John Paul II of 1988. The main thrust of this document is evangelization: "Each Christian, by virtue of baptism, is a missionary disciple to the extent that he or she has encountered the love of Christ Jesus."[13] *Praedicate Evangelium* states that since evangelization implies a fundamental option for the poor, it (Dicastery for Evangelization) organizes the World Day of the Poor (Article 53, #2).

---

[11] Pope Francis, *Evangelii Gaudium* (Vatican: Libreria Editrice Vaticana, 2013). See Nos 14 and 15.
[12] Pope Francis, *Praedicate Evangelium* (Vatican: Libreria Editrice Vaticana, 2022).
[13] Pope Francis, *Praedicate Evangelium*, No. 10.

The theme of the 16th Ordinary General Synod of Bishops, which will be concluded in October 2024, is: "For a Synodal Church: Communion, Participation and Mission." The very missionary nature of the Church is beautifully described in the preparatory document number 2: "A basic question prompts and guides us: How does this journeying together, which takes place today on different levels, from the local level to the universal one, allow the Church to proclaim the Gospel in accordance with the mission entrusted to her."

The time has come to think seriously about the mission commitment of the Church. The Church should move from *Missio Dei* to *Missio Ecclesiae*, from *Ad Gentes* to New Evangelization, and from *Missio inter Gentes* to *Missio cum Gentibus*.

Social Teaching and Mission

The social teaching of the Roman Catholic Church is an integral part of her evangelizing ministry. It seeks to proclaim the Gospel and make it present in the complex network of social relations. Through her social teaching, the Church attempts to interpret the social realities of the world in the light of the Gospel values and thus guide Christian behaviour, reminding Christians of their vocation as human beings created in the image and likeness of God.[14]

Pope John XXIII's encyclical, *Pacem in Terris* (Peace on Earth),[15] 1963, had a great impact on the formulation of some of the documents of the Second Vatican Council, including *Lumen Gentium* (LG number 36) and *Ad Gentes* (AG number 8). "Missionary activity is closely bound up too with human nature itself and its aspirations ... The Gospel has truly been a leaven of liberty and progress in human history, even in its temporal sphere, and always proves itself a leaven of brotherhood, of unity and of peace" (AG number 8). The Decree on Ecumenism, *Unitatis Redintegratio* (UR) numbers 4 and 12 speak about the need for dialogue and cooperation among Christians in the field of social commitments. A Research Seminar on "The Indian Church in the Struggle for a New Society" was held in Bangalore in 1981. Its aim was to clarify how the Church's mission and the struggle for justice and liberation are related to the full and final coming of God's reign and how the Church could contribute to it by joining the struggle to create a new society.[16]

---

[14] Thonippara Francis, "Pacem in Terris: New Perspectives, Dynamics and Orientations in the Social Teaching of the Catholic Church in the Context of Globalisation," in *Globalisation and Response of the Churches*, eds. Alphonsus D'Souza, O.L. Snaitang and Limatula Longkumer (Guwahati: North Eastern Social Research Centre, 2014), 60-61. Refer also, 61-79 for the full article.

[15] As the full title of the encyclical indicates, it appeals for the establishing of universal peace in truth, justice, charity and liberty. *Pacem in Terris: Encyclical of Pope John XXII on Establishing Universal Peace in Truth, Justice, Charity, and Liberty*, April 11, 1963.

[16] Kanjamala, *Paths of Mission in India Today*, 57.

Challenges

The shift from an emphasis on "no salvation outside the Church" to "salvation in all religious traditions" and the concept of "anonymous Christians" weakened the traditional understanding of the Catholic mission and missionary commitments. Anonymous Christianity means that a person, in God's grace, attains salvation outside of explicitly constituted Christianity. Catholic theologian Karl Rahner was the exponent of this concept. According to the concept of Anonymous Christianity, the "mystery of Christ" is contained in varying degrees in non-Christian religions. Therefore, salvation is also available in those other religions. To evaluate the mission in the changing scenario of India, the CBCI Commission for Proclamation and Communication met at Ishavani Kendra, Pune, in January 1994. A National Survey on Roman Catholic Mission was conducted as a preparation for the consultation in Pune. "The Second Vatican Council's teaching that God's saving love extends to all people (NA 1; AG 2; LG 8; GS 22) has been accepted by a majority of the respondents. About 66 percent of the clergy and 74 percent of the religious sisters maintain that all religions are paths of salvation for their sincere followers. In contrast, 16 percent of the clergy and sisters and 58 percent of the lay people subscribe to the view, widely prevalent earlier, that there is no salvation outside the boundaries of the visible Church."[17] However, more recent understandings and appreciation of other religions should not prevent one from his/her basic obligation of preaching the Good News to the ends of the world, a command given by Our Lord and Saviour Jesus Christ (Matt. 28,19-20; Mk 16, 15-18; Lk. 24, 47-48; and Jn 20, 21-23).

Conclusion

The twentieth century was a Christian century, and Christianity has become a truly global faith fulfilling its purpose recorded in Matthew 28:19, to "make disciples of all nations." Mission work is a constitutive element of the nature of the Church. *Ad Gentes* gave a new impulse to the missionary activity of the Church. Proclaiming and bearing witness to the Gospel are the first services Christians can render to the individual person and to the whole human race. There is no Church if there is no Mission. To become a true missionary Church, it has to overcome the dangers of intellectualism, formalism and immobilism. A true missionary Church is a transformation from clericalism to participation of the laity, from patriarchalism to women empowerment, from authoritarianism to service, from self-seeking to the common good and from institutional to community formation. Communion spirituality and servant model leadership are the needs of the hour for an effective witnessing of the Kingdom values.

---

[17] *Ibid.* 15.

Decolonial Reading of the Context of Mission in Northeast India

Taimaya Ragui

When people talk about Christian missions in northeast India (NEI),[1] the (immediate) tendency is to refer to the late nineteenth and early twentieth-century western missionaries and what they brought to help the region's tribal-indigenous communities grow and develop.[2] To understand Christian missions, one must also consider the growth of the church (as well as the expansion of church buildings and properties) among tribal-indigenous communities in the NE region. However, such a tendency implies a sense of colonial captivity in the discussion and practice of mission in/from NEI. The dominant voice-structure (that is, the colonial influence-tendency) takes precedence in formulating mission policies and strategies, while the voice from the margin, particularly the tribal-indigenous experience, is ignored or neglected. It also implies that tribal-indigenous communities' epistemic contributions are not valued in discussions of truth claims and the enterprise of Christian mission in/from NEI. However, there is a need to validate tribal-indigenous communities' everyday experiences while considering their context. This is meant to imply that the context of tribal-indigenous communities is no longer fixed in one place but rather is fluid. They now live in multiple contexts with the potential for multiple inputs from various geographical locations, historical specificities and cross-cultural experiences.

This contribution attempts to accomplish this through decolonial thinking while attempting to understand the context of the Christian mission in NEI, specifically within the Tangkhul Naga community, which is geographically located in Ukhrul district and other districts in Manipur, North-western Myanmar and several Indian cities. While discussing the context of mission in NEI, it raises concerns about the tendency to emulate the thinking and practise of Western missionaries and/or British ethnographers and their failure to understand the Tangkhul Naga's cultural context. This is not to entirely dismiss their contributions to advancement. However, it is to propose that there is also a need to consider the Tangkhul Naga's epistemic input, especially their experience, from multiple perspectives (that is, recognise input from multiple contexts). As a corrective to the Tangkhul Baptist approach to missions,[3] this

---

[1] Hereafter, the terms "Northeast India" will be referred to as NEI and "Northeast" as NE respectively.
[2] This paper acknowledges that the term tribe/tribal was imposed by colonials. It is used interchangeably with the term indigenous or indigenous communities. The terms "tribal" and "indigenous" are hyphenated here for two reasons: to acknowledge that they are indigenous to the Northeast India regions, and to correlate their experiences to those of other indigenous communities outside the region.
[3] Hereafter, the term Tangkhul community or church is used in reference to the thinking and practices of Tangkhul Baptist churches.

effort can be seen as a move away from conventional understanding and doing missions in/from NEI.⁴ This effort to reconsider Christian missions has its roots in the early twentieth century with "the rethinking group"⁵ and also tribal-indigenous efforts to contextualise theology in the late twentieth century.⁶

Methodology

In terms of methodology, this paper adopts (and adapts) Gerald M. Boodoo's concept of "decolonial thinking" of Christian mission.⁷ Boodoo argues for the importance of "decolonial thinking" and its ability to decolonize our theology while also "creating avenues for realistic and feasible epistemologies, active engagement and spiritualities."⁸ While he examines missions from a Caribbean perspective, his method can also be applied in the NEI context.⁹ When discussing decolonial mission thinking, he identifies three areas that require consideration. First, it is necessary to recognise that "modernity" (often associated with colonisation in the erstwhile western colonies/Majority world) has brought "a world system that for the first time in the history of [the] world has linked all (or virtually all) parts of the world and subsumed them into a connected system."¹⁰ In the case of the Tangkhul Naga, this means that with the arrival of Western missionaries and British colonisers in NEI, new cultural values were planted in the people's thinking and practices, undermining tribal-indigenous values. As their perceptions are merged or colonised by and with the colonial worldview, such input now influences how they think and act. Even after they have long been gone, tribal-indigenous communities are still being colonised in some ways.

---

⁴ In my region, we have a dominant approach to mission, that is, from the church to the world. This is to imply that mission is carried out from a supracultural perspective, with little constructive engagement with culture or context.
⁵ Again, this development is reminiscent of the International Missionary Council's general meeting in Tambaram, Madras, in 1938. See Thomas, M.M. "An Assessment of Tambaram's Contribution to the Search of the Asian Churches for an Authentic Selfhood." in *IRM* 77:307 (1988), 390–397. See also Richard, H.L. "Rethinking 'Rethinking.'" in *IJT* 45:1&1 (2003), 88-104.
⁶ See Shimreingam Shimray (ed.) *Tribal Theology: A Reader: Tribal Study Series No. 12* (Jorhat, Assam: Tribal Study Centre, 2003).
⁷ See Gerald M. Boodoo, "Spaces of Possibility: Contributions of Local Theologies," in *CTSA Proceedings* 74 (2019), 46-61; Gerald M. Boodoo, "Mission and Coloniality: Christianity and the Caribbean," in *Mission for Diversity: Exploring Christian Mission in the Contemporary World* (ed.) Elochukwu E. Uzukwu (Zurich: LIT, 2015), 68-75.
⁸ *Ibid.* 52.
⁹ See, for example, Shiluinla Jamir, *Embracing God's Beloved Community: Rethinking Mission in Asia during Covid-19 and Beyond* (n.p.: Asia CMS, 2020).
¹⁰ Boodoo, "Mission and Coloniality," 68. Cf. Anibal Quijano, "Coloniality of Power, Eurocentrism, and Social Classification," in *Coloniality at Large: Latin America and the Postcolonial Debate*, ed. Mabel Morana, Enrique Dussel and Carlos A. Jauregui (Durham, NC: Duke University Press 2008), 181-224.

Second, Boodoo claims that a "coloniality of power" "privileges and enshrines Euro-American thinking by constituting itself in all areas of life."[11] Western missionaries and British colonisers' local knowledge and histories are projected with "global designs."[12] In this context, it means that the Western missionary approach to mission (or ministry) shapes how it is perceived and practised. Such captivity pervades not only Christian missions but all aspects of life – and towers over them.

Third, decolonial thinking encourages "a new way of thinking" that "seeks to produce knowledge formed from the colonial difference."[13] Despite the obvious colonial tendency, they should not remain there, that is, continue to live in colonial legacy. Concerns arising from neglected areas, such as the tribal-indigenous experience, must be prioritised. The epistemic input – the tribal-indigenous experience – that comes from the Tangkhul Naga's multiple contexts is the colonial difference. This could be a corrective to the colonial tendency of viewing mission as "a movement taking place from centre to the periphery, and from the privileged to the marginalised of society."[14] This is a revision of the mission where Christian missions take place "from the margins."[15] What that tribal-indigenous experience entails for the Tangkhul Naga will be elaborated in the following section.

The Context of Tangkhul Naga

Tangkhul Christians' engagement with the question of mission context revolves around (mostly) church concerns while ignoring the tribal-indigenous community's epistemic input.[16] In contrast, this contribution hopes to address this concern/neglect by recognising the context of Christian missions within the Tangkhul Naga's multiple contexts. It entails investigating the question of mission context from various perspectives, namely the mission context of Tangkhul Naga in the pre-colonial and colonial, post-colonial and contemporary periods.

Pre-Colonial and Colonial Period

The question of mission context should begin at the intersection of the pre-colonial and colonial periods or between colonials and tribal-indigenous groups. The question of mission or its context arose with the arrival of Western

---

[11] *Ibid.* 68.
[12] Walter D. Mignolo, *Local Histories/Global Designs: Coloniality, Subaltern Knowledges, and Border Thinking* (Princeton: Princeton University Press, 2000), 17.
[13] Boodoo, "Mission and Coloniality," 68.
[14] Jooseop Keum, ed., *Together Towards Life*: *Mission and Evangelism in Changing Landscapes* (Geneva: WCC, 2013), 5.
[15] *Ibid.*
[16] While ecclesial concerns should be prioritised, this should not come at the expense of ignoring the tribal-indigenous experience of the people. In another context, I argued for the importance of taking the ecclesial context into account when doing a tribal-theological reading of the Bible. Taimaya Ragui, "A Tribal-Theological Reading of the Bible," in *Journal of Tribal Studies* 26:1&2 (2021), 1-20.

missionaries in NEI. In this context, Christian mission is defined as sending or reaching out to a group of people of other faiths, that is, religious beliefs other than Christianity. So, when discussing the context of the Tangkhul Naga mission, it is only natural to begin with the tribal-indigenous community's geographical location and the colonial perception of the tribal-indigenous people and their culture.

When William Pettigrew (1869-1943), the first Western missionary among Manipur's tribal-indigenous communities, reported on the beginning of his missionary work, he geographically located them as follows: "...the missionary was allowed to commence work amongst the Tangkhul Nagas inhabiting the hills forty miles to the north-east of the capital, but still in the state of Manipur."[17] In the same report, he called the Tangkhuls "uncivilized", "demon worshippers" and "superstitious". These derogatory words were followed by unpleasant remarks about how difficult it had been to work among the Tangkhuls. Looking at his work as a favour to the Tangkhuls, he went to them with a strong sense of a superiority complex or a sense of the utter complexity of his mission task.[18] This is evident in his assessment of his missionary work in Ukhrul: "It has been no small task during the past year to make these village people, and Ukhrul in particular, understand that it was for their good the missionary has come amongst them."[19]

His negative attitude towards the Tangkhuls did not change even after years of working with them. This is evident in the following report: "Like the rest of the Nagas in Assam, they are animistic in their worship, very superstitious, and addicted to *'zu'* drinking to a great extent."[20] If his report is taken literally, Tangkhuls are portrayed as a relatively insignificant ethnic group. They are classified as "animistic" and "demon worshippers"; and thus categorised as a group of people who worship nature, animals and inanimate objects. And because they are labelled as ignorant or irrational groups of people, their way of life and culture are deemed insignificant. Furthermore, if readers were to believe Pettigrew, the tribal-indigenous community was projected as a group of alcoholics, as he failed to recognise *zu* (*khor*) or rice beer as their staple food.

Even after a decade of living with the Tangkhuls, there is a lack of respect for tribal-indigenous culture.[21] His report showed no expression of love or care for the tribal-indigenous community. And rather than embracing their way of life,

---

[17] He began his missionary work in Ukhrul in 1896. William Pettigrew, "Ukhrul – 1896," *The Baptist Missionary Magazine* 77:7 (1897), 325.

[18] This is clear from his letters and reports. He only discusses his work or what he has accomplished. Apart from derogatory remarks about the tribal-indigenous people, he never expresses love or concern for them.

[19] Pettigrew, "Ukhrul – 1896," 326.

[20] William Pettigrew, "Report from the Tangkhul Naga Field," in *The Assam of the American Baptist Foreign Mission Society: Minutes, Resolutions and Historical of the Fifth Triennial Conference, February 11-19, 1899*. (Calcutta: The Baptist Mission Press, 1899), 50-55.

[21] William Pettigrew, "Kathe Kasham: The 'Soul Departure' Feast as Practised by the Tangkhul Nagas, Manipur, Assam," in *Journal of Proceedings of the Asiatic Society of Bengal* 5 (1909), 37-46.

he despised their understanding of reality. Pettigrew saw himself as a "light bearer" on a "civilising mission".[22] This is reflected in the following statement about his work:

> When the writer commenced his work in Manipur 33 years ago, and tried to devise ways and means whereby the gross ignorance might be dispelled from the minds of the young men and women, opposition met him at every turn, and only persistent plodding in the face of it won the day. Today we see the great and sincere desire in [sic] the part of all, both men and women, to do all in their power to bring their people up to that standard of life whereby they will be able to teach and train themselves for the great service awaiting them in the future.[23]

The above description implies that the tribal-indigenous way of life will be abandoned in favour of (early) twentieth-century Western civilization. As a result, when Pettigrew and his wife, Alice, began their work among the Tangkhuls, they started by establishing a school. This enabled them to preach God's Word and impart Western education.[24] They were spreading a Western way of life alongside the gospel, implicitly undermining and discriminating against tribal-indigenous knowledge and culture.

British administrators and/or ethnographers also contributed to the Western way of life and civilization in the region. T.C. Hodson identified a group of Tangkhuls in Myanmar while giving a demographic description of Tangkhuls in the Naga Tribes of Manipur: "On the east they touch the frontier Upper Burma (Upper Chindwin District) and the Somra group of villages, which is outside the territory of the State of Manipur, is of Tangkhul origin and is in contact [with] Singpho tribes on the east and north-east."[25] While Tangkhuls also live in Somra, they are now under Myanmar's demographic control. Following British administrative control of the NE region, their lands were divided based on administrative requirements. The Kubbo valley was given to Myanmar (Burma in the colonial report) in 1834, and "the boundary line north of it should be drawn so as to separate the Ungoching hills in the east (which falls in Burma) from the continuation of the western range of the Yumadoung or Malain hills, which are in Manipur."[26] As a result of this administrative arrangement, the Tangkhuls were geographically divided into separate districts in British India. This hegemonic control of demographic location was extended to socio-cultural values with colonial values absorbing the tribal-indigenous culture. According to Frederick S. Down,

---

[22] See, for example, Carey A. Watt and Michael Mann, eds. *Civilizing Missions in Colonial and Postcolonial South Asia: From Improvement to Development, Second Edition* (London: Anthem Press, 2011).
[23] William Pettigrew, "Appendix – II: A Great Convention in Manipur," in *Rev. William Pettigrew: A Pioneer Missionary of Manipur,* ed. PCCC. (Imphal, Manipur: Fraternal Green Cross, 1996), xxv.
[24] Pettigrew, "Ukhrul – 1896," 326. See also William Pettigrew, *Tangkhul Primer I,* Rev. S.J. Duncan. illus. Y.K. Shimray (Ukhrul: S. Kanrei, [1897]).
[25] T.C. Hodson, *The Naga Tribes of Manipur* (London: Macmillan and Co., Limited, 1911), 2.
[26] E.W. Dun, *Gazetteer of Manipur* (Delhi: Manas Publication, 1992), 1-2.

The scattered village-states, each with its own sub-culture, had provided the foundation for the traditional socio-cultural institutions and defined the horizons of the people's worldview. This traditional system could not survive under the centralized British administration and jurisprudence.[27]

It means the tribal-indigenous culture could not withstand the onslaught of colonial influence and dictation. "Through their organisation, literature, educational activities and ideology, the Christian missions provided the tribes with the skills and perspectives necessary to maintain distinct identities," they say.[28] Instead of assisting the Tangkhuls in seeing their cultural ingenuity, the idea of cultural inferiority (in comparison to the colonisers) was implanted in their minds.

Such behaviour, one could argue, is typical of British administrators and/or ethnographers. J.H. Hutton writes about head-hunting practises among the Angami Nagas in another context.

It is agreed by all Angamis, as well as by other Nagas, that head taking was essential to marriage in so far that a buck who had taken no head, and would not wear the warriors' dress at festival, not only found it exceedingly difficult to get any girl with pretensions to good looks or to self-respect to marry him, but was held up to ridicule by all the girls of his clan.[29]

Tribal-indigenous practices are at risk of being misunderstood because of such skewed perceptions. According to P.K. Misra, Hutton's description led other Britishers to believe that "the people in the Naga hills ... were all wild savages, continuously at war with each other, seeking all the 'heads' of their enemies as trophies."[30] In addition to promoting the superiority of their culture and civilization, they were misinforming those in the outside world about the tribal-indigenous community and their way of life.

Post-Colonial Period

The negative perception of the tribals created by the Western missionaries and colonisers was uncritically carried forward in the subsequent period (and to a large extent, even in the present period). The question of the mission's context has largely remained within colonial thinking (especially in the ecclesial setting). While some changes have begun in academia, tribal-indigenous churches remain rooted in the colonial framework. Such confinement is common not only in the church but also in other fields of study.

---

[27] Frederick S. Downs, "Baptist and Tribal Identity in North East India," in *American Baptist Quarterly* 20:1 (2001), 63.
[28] Downs, "Baptist and Tribal Identity in North East India," 63. See also Frederick S. Downs, "Christianity as a Tribal Response to Change in North-East India," in *Missiology* 8 (Oct. 1980), 407-416; Frederick S. Downs, "Administrators, Missionaries and a World Turned Upside Downs: Christianity as a Tribal Response to Change in North East India," in *Indian Church History Review* 15 (December 1981), 99-113.
[29] J.H. Hutton, *The Angami Nagas* (London: Macmillan, 1921), 165.
[30] P.K. Misra, "J.H. Hutton and Colonial Ethnography of North-East India," in *North-East India: A Handbook of Anthropology*, ed. T.B. Subba (Noida: Orient Blackswan, 2012), 63.

I begin by arguing that the colonial description and understanding of tribal-indigenous communities are carried forward in central-state documents in Independent India, as well as in the works of local Christian workers and writers. The tribal-indigenous communities in India are classified as "Scheduled Castes" and "Scheduled Tribes," with the assumed understanding that they are a group of people who belong to the "backward classes."[31] A similar description of the tribal-indigenous community found on a government website states as follows:

> The Ukhrul district lies in the north-eastern corner of Manipur State and it extends between latitudes of 24° 29' and 25° 42 N and longitudes of 94° 30 and 94° 45 E approximately (including areas of Kamjong district). Ukhrul District is bounded by Myanmar in the East, Kamjong District in the South, Kangpokpi and Senapati Districts in the West and Nagaland State in the North. The total area of the district including Kamjong was 4544 sq.km. In 2011 Census report, the district has 213 inhabited villages and no uninhabited village. The inhabitants are mostly local tribal people.[32]

This demographic description is consistent with the tribal-indigenous community's colonial categorization. What it falls short of is the exclusion of Tangkhul Nagas, who live in Myanmar's north-western region (also known as Somra Tangkhul).[33] It also differs from tribal-indigenous peoples' perception of themselves. Policymakers in India have failed to recognize that using terms like tribe or tribals is problematic. Raile Rocky contends that when British administrators and/or ethnographers collected data on tribal-indigenous people, they used terms and connotations that are synonymous with "being backward, uncivilised and barbarous."[34] While their work aided them in their administration or classification of people groups, they brought with them strong "cultural supremacy" and cultural biases.[35] In addition to the tribal-indigenous community's derogatory categorization, it worked against how they identify themselves. The word tribe/tribal is not preferred. They prefer to be addressed by the name of their ethnic group, such as Tangkhul, Ao, Angami, Kuki, Mizos, Khasis and so on.[36] Even in terms of conception, the Indian constitution's definition of tribal-indigenous communities as tribals is flawed. They are defined as a homogeneous community that does not belong to either the Hindu or Muslim communities, as well as those who are economically disadvantaged and socially marginalized. What is left out of that definition is that tribal-indigenous communities have their own traditional religion (or folk religion) that is

---

[31] Government of India, *The Constituent of India* (New Delhi: Government of India, 1949), 163, 165.
[32] "Demography", accessed June 7, 2021, https://ukhrul.nic.in/demography/.
[33] In the contemporary context, they also reside in other parts of Manipur, such as in Chandel, Senapati and Thoupal. See also https://www.go-myanmar.com/homalin (Accessed on June 8, 2021).
[34] R.L. Rocky, "Tribes and Tribal Studies in North East: Deconstructing the Politics of Colonial Methodology" in *Journal of Tribal Intellectual Collective India* 1:2 (2013), 25-37.
[35] Rocky, "Tribes and Tribal Studies in North East," 7.
[36] A. Wati Longchar, *An Emerging Asian Theology: Tribal Theology Issues, Method and Perspective* (Jorhat: TSC, 2000), 2.

sustainable in terms of the principality. They also have their own civilization distinct from Western missionaries and British colonials.

Their ethnic identity has traditionally been limited to the family, clans of the community, and the village to which they belong.[37] Understanding a shared identity, such as Nagas or other collective names, is a relatively new development. For example, when Western missionaries and British colonizers arrived in the region, there was little, if any, sense of Naga identity. The colonials, who themselves were not tribals, provided the collective identity.[38] There was some recognition of the shared dialect, religious values, social norms and practices of people living in a specific geographical area.[39] However, such shared or collective cultural identity was not as strong.[40] Their cultural engagement and development context was limited to a village and its neighbouring villages. As a result, their interaction with the outside world was limited to neighbouring villages, whether through war, conflict or trade. Hence, when western missionaries and British colonizers arrived in the area, they appeared to be isolated or disconnected from the rest of the world. Unfortunately, many tribal-indigenous writers regard this colonial description of the Tangkhul Nagas as a reliable source.

After the last missionary left Manipur in 1954, locals continued the missionary-evangelistic, educational and translation work. When the Christian baton was passed down to the locals, one of the first things they did was make the Bible available in the Tangkhul language. Their desire to translate the Bible into the local language (Ukhrul-Hunphun dialect) coincided with their desire to spread/preach the gospel.[41] Pettigrew chose the Ukhrul-Hunphun dialect to be the Tangkhuls' common language. Despite being aware of the existence of several dialects (about 150 villages), he made the strategic decision to make the Ukhrul dialect the Tangkhuls' common language.[42] However, no attempt was made in such efforts (whether in Tangkhul Bible translation or Tangkhul dictionary) to relate with other Tangkhul dialects, despite each village having its own distinct dialect. Pettigrew's primary goal was to teach locals to read and write while maintaining colonial values.[43] Other village dialects were overlooked

---

[37] S.M. Duby, "Inter-Ethnic Alliance, Tribal Movements and Integration in North-East India," in *Tribal Movements in India,* Vol. 1, ed. K.S. Singh (Manohar Publications, New Delhi:1982), 4.
[38] Duby, "Inter-Ethnic Alliance, Tribal Movements and Integration in North-East India," 4.
[39] Downs, "Baptist and Tribal Identity in North East India," 64.
[40] Hodson, *The Naga Tribes of Manipur,* 81. See also William Carlson Smith, *The Ao Naga Tribe of Assam: A Study in Ethnology and Sociology* (London: Macmillan and Co., Limited, 1925), 52.
[41] See Ningatei Rungsung, trans. *Kathara Bible,* Styl. Y.K. Shimray (Bangalore: Bible Society of India, 1977).
[42] William Pettigrew, *Tāngkul Nāga Grammar and Dictionary (Ukhrul Dialect) With Illustrative Sentences* (Shillong: The Assam Secretariat Printing Office, 1918), p. 1.
[43] See Pettigrew, *Tangkhul Primer I.*

in the effort to make the Ukhrul dialect the common language.[44] This resulted in the gradual extinction of many Tangkhul village dialects. Though his work on the Tangkhul language is lauded, the capitalization of the Ukhrul dialect has resulted in either "an amalgamation of multiple vocabularies into one language (that is, one common language), or a slow endangering of Tangkhul village languages (that is, multiple languages)."[45]

Locals began questioning the legitimacy of continuous colonial captivity two decades after all Western missionaries had left. Locals began to ask, according to M. Horam, "If the Western Christians can sing, dance and drink and yet be Christians, why should not the Nagas have their own way of life and still be good Christians?"[46] One could argue that this has its roots in the rethinking movement in the early twentieth century and corresponds with the emergence of liberation theologies in Latin America and the Majority World. Growing awareness of tribal issues and discussions about the need for contextual theologies in NEI began in the 1970s.[47]

The rethinking movement is a reaction to the dominant presence – dominance of Western missionaries and Western thought. According to it, "the Christian evangel could not function normally in India until it is rescued from the ecclesial overgrowth that has come from the West and is adapted to the great religious heritage of this ancient land of religions."[48] It reacted to the Eurocentric view of Christianity and the church, which held that Western thinking represented the best form of Christian faith and organisation and that the Indian church should respond to such an outlook.[49] In other words, there was an assumption that the Indian Christian church should be structured in accordance with Western thought. This new development, as was mentioned earlier, brings to mind the general meeting of the International Missionary Council that took place in

---

[44] Tangkhul language/dialects are listed by UNESCO as "vulnerable" or endangered languages. This is cause for concern on our part. It is too soon to suggest a quick fix. However, it appears that an indigenous framework of the Ukhrul dialect and other Tangkhul village dialects is required. Accessed October 11, 2019, https://tangkhulonline.com/google-earth-celebrates-indigenous-languages/.
[45] Taimaya Ragui, "Tangkhul Language or Languages?" *Ukhrul Times* (August 24, 2021) https://ukhrultimes.com/tangkhul-language-or-languages/.
[46] M. Horam, *Social and Cultural Life of Nagas* (Delhi: P.R. Publishing Corporation, 1977), 14.
[47] Akala Imchen, "Development of Indigenous Theology in North East India: An Appraisal," in *Doing Indigenous Theology in Asia: Towards New Frontiers*, eds. Hrangthan Chhungi, M.M. Ekka, and Wati Longchar (Nagpur, India: NCCI/GTC/SCEPTRE, 2012), 1-24.
[48] D.M. Devasahayam and A.N. Sundarisanam, "Preface to the Second Edition," in *Rethinking Christianity in India, Second Edition*, ed. G.V. Job, et al (Madras: A.N. Sundarisanam, 1939), iii.
[49] Stephen Neil was referring to the mindset of the late nineteenth century Western missionaries and their perception of the Indian Church. Stephen Neil, *A History of Christianity in India: The Beginnings to AD 1707* (Cambridge: CUP, 1984), 386.

Tambaram, Madras, in 1938.[50] It emphasized the importance of grounding the Christian faith in the context of the people, that is, Indian Christian thinking should emerge from the Indian context.[51]

Similarly, in the context of NEI, individuals such as Gordon Jones and Jonathan H. Thumra provided early impetus for a relevant theology (that is, tribal theology). Jones challenged the tribes to "understand the Gospel in its essentials and to interpret it, to translate it, into terms that meet the needs of the people of [NE] India."[52] He proposes that the tribals view Christ as the conqueror, the "Christus Victor," in order to develop a relevant theology for NEI. This was said with the understanding that Jesus is the conqueror and liberator of all evils, whether they are social, political or both. The figure of Jesus is portrayed as the victor over tribal issues such as oppression, suppression, subjugation and so on. Similarly, Jonathan H. Thumra argued for the importance of contextual theologies in NEI.[53] Around this time, tribal-indigenous communities in NEI began to have reservations about the dominant theology, particularly those associated with Western missionaries and colonialism. This emphasis on contextual theological reflection was deemed significant because tribal-indigenous churches' thinking and practises were perceived as "too superficial" or unconnected with their context and culture.[54] These efforts sought to make the Christian faith more culturally relevant and relatable to the general masses. This tribal-indigenous pursuit was not a one-off occurrence. According to Nalini Natarjan, the desire to express one's Christian beliefs through cultural heritage was also seen among the Khasi tribe.[55] These efforts maintain that what was perceived as Christianity or Christian theology in NEI was irrelevant to the people's context and experience. Renthy Keitzar held the opinion that,

> The message of the gospel has not gone deep into the cultural life of tribal Christianity; it is not rooted firmly in the tribal soil; it is still a xerox-copy of American Baptist Christianity, or a duplicate of western Presbyterianism or a

---

[50] See M.M. Thomas, "An Assessment of Tambaram's Contribution to the Search of the Asian Churches for an Authentic Selfhood," in *IRM* 77:307 (1988), 390–397. See also Richard, "Rethinking 'Rethinking,'" 88-104.

[51] See Norman Goodall and et al, ed., *A Decisive Hour for the Christian Mission, The EACC 1959 and the John R. Mott Memorial Lectures* (London: SCM Press, 1960).

[52] Gordon Jones, "Good News for North-East India," in *ETC Magazine* (1971-72), 4-8. See also Gordon Jones, "Good News for North-East India," in *Good News for North East India: A Theological Reader*, ed. Renthy Keitzar (Assam: The India Literature Centre, 1995), 1-7.

[53] Jonathan H. Thumra, "Communicating Good News through Theological Education," *The Baptist Leader* 21.4 (1973): 5-7. See also Jonathan H. Thumra, "The Triumph of the Gospel" in *Good News for North East India: A Theological Reader,* ed. Renthy Keitzar (Assam: The Christian Literature Centre, 1995), 216-219. See also J.H. Thumra, "The Triumph of the Gospel (Romans 1:16)," in *The Baptist Leader* 29 (1980), 7-9.

[54] Renthy Keitzar, "Tribal Perspective in Biblical Hermeneutics Today," in *IJT* 31.3-4 (1982), 310.

[55] Nalini Natarjan, *The Missionary Among the Khasis* (Gauhati: United Publishers, 1977), 193. For an example in the Mizo context, see K. Thanzauva, ed. *Towards a Tribal Theology: The Mizo Perspective* (Aizawl: Mizoram Theological Conference, 1989).

carbon-copy of the charismatic movement of Pentecostalism, or even a replica of Roman Catholics of pre-Vatican II.[56]

This implied that tribal-indigenous churches in NEI were carrying on the legacy of Western missionaries. Tribal-indigenous scholars today day argue that the prevalent theology of the time did not connect with the traditional worldview.[57] Such an argument confronted the preaching and practises of tribal-indigenous churches, which appeared to prioritise only the spiritual aspect of the tribal-indigenous community/church.

Unfortunately, this criticism of tribal-indigenous churches offended or made many church leaders uncomfortable. As a result, rather than seeing the discussion of contextual theology in NEI as beneficial or the way forward, some have labelled it a "compromise and syncretism" of traditional religion-culture with Christian belief.[58] Some theological educators have gone so far as to call such theological pursuits "unbiblical" – and thus detrimental to the church.[59] Gradually, a schism developed between what is preached and practised in the church and what is taught and discussed in academia. The context of mission is then understood differently by two different groups of people: (i) academia which responds to the tribal-indigenous community's socio-political issues and concerns, and (ii) the church which caters to the people's spiritual needs while situating itself in the ecclesial context/setting.

Contemporary Period

Many Christian workers or church-based writers still struggle to move past their admiration of Western missionaries and colonisers – and what they claimed to have achieved for and within the Tangkhul community. This admiration stems from their assumption that the Western missionaries and colonisers were saviours. Thus, they continue perpetuating the derogatory reference to their people and culture, with their high regard for the Western missionaries and colonials to whom they feel indebted.

They had difficulty breaking free from colonial captivity within the context of the church because the colonial framework has been so firmly embedded. In light of this, it is important to remember what Keitzar had to say: "The message of the Gospel has not gone deep into the cultural life of tribal Christianity; it is not rooted firmly in the tribal soil."[60] This form of captivity is reflected in the way in which they uncritically adopt Western missionary teachings and practises in the church (that is, the dominant voice), while at the same time remaining critical of the input from the tribal-indigenous experience and culture (that is, the voice of the margins). For instance, Gangmumei Kamei suggests that local

---

[56] Keitzar, "Tribal Perspective in Biblical Hermeneutics Today," 310.
[57] A. Wati Longchar, "The Need for Doing Tribal Theology," in *Tribal Theology: A Reader*, ed. Shimreingam Shimray (Assam: TSC, 2003), 1-16.
[58] Renthy Keitzar, "Theology Today," in *In Search of Praxis Theology for the Nagas*, ed. V.K. Nuh (New Delhi: Regency, 2003), 21.
[59] See, for example, Visakuolie Vakha, "Jesus Christ in Tribal Theology: A Critique," in *Perspectives: Current Issues in Theological Thinking*, ed. Akheto Sumi (Mokokchung, Nagaland: Jongshinokdang Trust, 2002), 64-81.
[60] Keitzar, "Tribal Perspective in Biblical Hermeneutics Today," 310.

writers lack "criticality" when they write about William Pettigrew because they are "overwhelmed by admiration" for the Western missionary and what he did for them.⁶¹ Most of the articles and books about Pettigrew fall into this category; more specifically, while they express gratitude towards the Western missionaries and colonials, they fail to be critical of their contributions.⁶²

On the socio-political front, there has been significant socio-political unrest in NEI – and within the Tangkhul community. This unrest dates back to the beginning of the century. John Thomas asserts that "[The tribal-indigenous communities] did not want to have to do with a [socio-religious hierarchy] and wanted to be defined as a 'nation' in their own right."⁶³ By the 1980s, a number of NE ethnic groups had begun to identify with their own unique ethnic-national identities. This occurred first among the Nagas in the 1920s,⁶⁴ then among the Mizos in the 1960s, the Bodos and Khasis in the 1970s and so on.⁶⁵ Such a socio-political aspiration continues to be a current pursuit for the vast majority of ethnic groups, if not all of them, which invites socio-political movements throughout the region. In examining the context of mission in NEI, it is important to consider both the spiritual needs of the people and the reality that people are rising up and taking up arms against the government. It can be inferred from this that the ecclesiastical experience of the tribal people is subsumed within the aforementioned socio-political reality (that is, they are interconnected). Therefore, when discussing the context of Christian mission in NEI, it is important to take into account the context of the resistance.

At the socio-cultural level, one can make the case that the concerns of India's tribal-indigenous communities and other minority groups are being ignored on a systematic level. This kind of disregard was not only common in the past; it is still the case today. This fact is becoming increasingly obvious as tribal-indigenous communities from the NEI move to urban areas on the Indian mainland.⁶⁶ They become targets of "racism, sexual assault, [and] class exploitation" while they are looking for jobs, trying to improve their lives or pursuing higher education.⁶⁷ This is made clear by the number of cases of racial discrimination and hate crimes that have been reported (as well as those that have

---

⁶¹ Gangmumei Kamei, "Preface" in *Rev. William Pettigrew*, i.
⁶² See, for example, Pettigrew, William. *Forty Years in Manipur Assam* (ed.) Jonah M. Solo and K. Mahangthei. Imphal, Manipur: Mrs. M. Asenath and Mrs. K. Ruth, 1986; PCCC, ed. *William Pettigrew: A Pioneer Missionary of Manipur* (Imphal, Manipur: Fraternal Green Cross, 1996). See also A. S. Shimreiwung, "Pettigrew's Children: Tracing the History of Print Culture in Tangkhul Language," in *Journal of North East India Studies*, 3:2 (2013), 70-81; Shirik, Sochanngam. "Revisiting William Pettigrew's Legacy: A Missional Lesson for the Contemporary Church," in *Baptist News*, 68:3 (2017), 39-44.
⁶³ John Thomas, *Evangelising the Nation: Religion and the Formation of Naga Political Identity* (New Delhi: Routledge, 2016), 195.
⁶⁴ "Memorandum to the Simon Commission, 1929."
⁶⁵ Thomas, *Evangelising the Nation*, 194.
⁶⁶ See, for example, Haksar, Nadita. *The Exodus is not Over: Migrations from the Ruptured Homelands of Northeast India* (New Delhi: Speaking Tiger, 2016).
⁶⁷ *Ibid.* 1.

not been reported) against people from NEI in various parts of the country. According to the findings of a recent investigation carried out by the Indian Council for Social Science Research (ICSSR), "A series of attacks were reported in various parts of the country where people from the region were 'harassed, abused, and traumatised.'"[68] As a result of the outbreak of the coronavirus pandemic (Covid-19), the frequency of such crimes has increased. It is believed that this was because the victim's physical appearance is similar to that of Chinese people. Regrettably, most crimes committed against tribal-indigenous communities have not been solved. Even the offenses that were prioritised for prosecution by the central government, according to Sukanya Singha, are still only recorded on paper.[69] This modern reality of hate crimes and racial discrimination experienced by tribal-indigenous communities from NEI should not be overlooked when we articulate Christian mission. NEI students, professionals, migrant workers and others who are pursuing higher education, looking for better jobs and making a living in the cities face this ethnic injustice on a daily basis. This recommendation is also a call to the tribal-indigenous communities and churches both within and outside of NEI to respond to the social reality faced by the members of their church who live in the cities.

Mission in/from Multiple Contexts

The western missionaries and colonizers brought with them not only a Christian belief system but also their own cultural values that were prevalent at the time. As a result of their arrival and continued presence, a socio-religious system was introduced that eroded the tribal-indigenous people's cultural values. This perception continues to influence and permeate its way into tribal-indigenous communities' thinking and doing. To a large extent, members of the Tangkhul community continue to unquestioningly embrace the socio-cultural values of the Global North; in other words, they are enamoured with colonial values. According to Boodoo's interpretation, colonial values are "enshrined" as the fundamental principles that continue to govern their way of thinking and their methods of operation.[70] The tragic reality of such captivity is that people would have a negative attitude toward socio-cultural values that are indigenous in nature or origin but would readily accept values that colonisers imposed.

At the level of practical application, this pervasive disregard for tribal-indigenous values is accompanied by a propensity to divide the sacred from the secular. The sacred or spiritual refers to activities and events that take place within the church. They equate activities associated with the church, such as prayer, worship, devotion, preaching and so on, with the sacred. The world

---

[68] Vijaita Singh, "Northeast Citizens Faced Racial Discrimination Amid Covid-19 Outbreak, says Govt. Study" accessed June 30, 2021, https://www.thehindu.com/news/national/other-states/northeast-citizens-faced-racial-discrimination-amid-covid-19-outbreak-says-govt-study/article34303162.ece.
[69] Sukanya Singha, "Governments Have Failed to Address Racial Abuse of People from the Northeast", accessed June 30, 2021, https://thewire.in/rights/governments-have-failed-to-address-racial-abuse-of-people-from-the-northeast.
[70] Boodoo, "Mission and Coloniality," 68.

outside of the church, including social, political, and community service, as well as other aspects of society, is regarded as part of the secular aspect of society.[71] The concerns of the secular world are frequently disregarded, or disregarded entirely, by the church. The church does not consider the context of the secular world to be part of its ministry or mission. However, the church needs to make amends for the way it has neglected the so-called secular concerns for so long. The tribal-indigenous experience is primarily situated in these secular concerns; to put it another way, the activities that tribal-indigenous people engage in on a daily basis are located in the secular world. If this is the case, as demonstrated in the preceding analytical description, I recommend considering the multiple contexts of the Tangkhul Naga. Namely, we should trace the historical particularities of the arrival and dominance of the missionaries-colonials in the Tangkhul inhabited areas, identify the continuing legacy of missionaries-colonials or colonialism of the tribal-indigenous community by those in the Global North, and pay attention to the contemporary context of the tribal-indigenous community.[72] If we do this, we will be better able to understand the colonial difference in the context of the mission; more specifically, we will be able to capture the colonial difference if we consider the multiple contexts rather than locating ourselves in just one context.

To decolonize the mission with multi-contextual concerns is to strive for more than just the contextual-cultural concerns of the tribal-indigenous community. It is just as much to affirm what the Commission on World Mission and Evangelism (CWME) argued in Together Towards Life: "Mission from the margins calls for an understanding of the complexities of power dynamics, global systems and structures, and local contextual realities."[73] In this particular instance, it is imperative that consideration be given to the voices that are typically disregarded by the privileged or the dominant voice. To reiterate, this does not imply that the biblical framework or its rootedness in the Bible is being ignored in any way. Instead, it is to argue for the need to retain an argument of biblical concern that captures the concerns of the minority, the downtrodden or people from the margins of society; in other words, the Bible itself endorses the need to contextualize.[74] This entails agreeing that there is a pressing requirement

---

[71] Ragui, Taimaya. "The Crisis of the Divide Between Secular and Sacred" *Ukhrul Times* (September 17, 2021) https://ukhrultimes.com/the-crisis-of-the-divide-between-secular-and-sacred/.

[72] In another context, I argued for the historical distinctiveness of the (Tangkhul) confessing community's emergence in the pre-missionary, missionary, post-missionary, and contemporary periods. See Taimaya Ragui, "Cultural Interpretation as a Theological Task in Northeast India," in *Christianity, Ethnicity and Cultural Identity in Northeast India* (Oxford: Regnum Books International), *forthcoming*.

[73] Keum, ed., *Together Towards Life*, p. 15.

[74] According to Dean Flemming, contextualization is seen at two levels: first, it gives "stories of contextualization" where "Jesus and the apostles tailor the gospel message to address different groups of people" and second, "the New Testament writings are themselves examples of the church's theological task." Dean Flemming, *Contextualization in the New Testament: Patterns for Theology and Mission* (Downers Grove, Illinois: InterVarsity Press, 2005), 15.

to recoup what Jesus said and did at the outset of his ministry. Jesus, while proclaiming to be filled with the Spirit, said, "The Spirit of the Lord is upon me, because he has anointed me to bring good news to the poor. He has sent me to proclaim release to the captives and recovery of sight to the blind, to let the oppressed go free, to proclaim the year of the Lord's favour."[75] Jesus did not come to this earth to serve the wealthy or those in privileged positions; rather, he came to set free those in society who were less well-off or neglected. In this instance, and in light of the context of the early church, the term "poor" would function as "a cypher for those of low status, for those excluded according to normal canons of status honour in Mediterranean world."[76] It is to argue that "Jesus' mission is directed to the poor – defined not merely in subjective, spiritual or personal, economic terms, but in the holistic sense of those who are for any of a number of socio-religious reasons, relegated to positions outside the boundaries of God's people."[77] In addition, the passage suggests that "Jesus accomplished this mission by opting to be with the marginalized people of his time, not out of paternalistic charity but because their situations testified to the sinfulness of the world and their yearnings for life pointed to God's purposes."[78] If this is the case, then it is only right that we take into account the multiple contexts of the tribal-indigenous community where Tangkhul Nagas are dominated, neglected and held captive.

Conclusion

Examining the environment in which the Tangkhul Nagas carried out their mission demonstrates beyond a reasonable doubt that they are members of a less privileged segment of Indian society. They are a community that is still being colonized in one form or another; they are a community that is fighting for their rights to be recognized with their ethnic identity; and they are a community that bears the brunt of the oppression caused by the dominant groups, religions and structures that make up Indian society. However, the tribal-indigenous community as a whole has the propensity to be associated with the privileged or the socio-religious practices of the dominant structure. This tendency is fairly widespread. Their adoration of all things colonial continues to dominate their way of thinking, including how they approach mission work in or from NEI. As a result of the influence of the rethinking movement, the echo of the Tambaram meeting, and the emergence of contextual theologies in NEI, the context of Christian missions is currently being understood in a manner that is increasingly multi-contextual – or so the current contribution contends. It has been suggested that taking into account the tribal-indigenous perspective and the various

---

[75] Verses 16b-20 present "the address-response cycle" where "vv. 18-19 are framed by vv. 16b-17 on the one end, and v. 20 on the other." Joel B Green, *The Gospel of Luke, NICNT* (Grand Rapids, Mich.: Eerdmans, 1997), 209. Note: Cf. Luke 4: 18-19. Unless otherwise noted, all Scripture quotations are from the New Revised Standard Version (NRSV).
[76] Green, *The Gospel of Luke,* p. 211.
[77] *Ibid.*
[78] Keum, ed., *Together Towards Life*, p. 15.

contexts of the Tangkhul Naga is the most crucial step. In light of this, it is necessary to consider the margins' context on multiple levels.

Whither Theological Formation in India?

Chongpongmeren Jamir

In India, reflection on the condition and prospect of theological education is a well-trodden path. The earliest systematic inquiry into the question was made in 1930-1931 by the Commission on Christian Higher Education in India and Burma of the International Missionary Council (IMC). A few years later, following discussions on the issue in the IMC Tambaram in 1938, the National Christian Council of India, Burma and Ceylon (hereafter NCC) constituted a commission to investigate the state of theological education in India. These commissions called for a united effort by churches of different traditions towards providing quality theological education and the development of indigenous models of theological education that cater to the needs of the Indian churches and missions. The workings of these commissions also show that the importance of theological formation was embedded in the IMC process in India. This contribution discusses the influence of the IMC process, both past and present, on theological formation in India, reflecting on which, it attempts to discern some markers for the future of theological education in the region. It argues that theological educators and institutions need to work together towards setting common standards for theological education in India and to play the prophetic role of preparing/equipping the whole people of God to effectively engage with contemporary realities in society. Towards this end, first, it highlights the influence of the discussions and initiatives of the IMC process on the development of theological education in India. Second, it outlines the current state of theological seminaries/institutions in the region. Finally, it reflects on the future of theological formation in India in the light of the findings of the regional consultation of the IMC/CWME Centenary Study Process.

The IMC and Theological Education in India

There was already a great emphasis on the importance of the theological formation of missionaries in Edinburgh 1910. Two of the major commission reports at the conference, Commission III and Commission V, deal with issues of theological formation. Commission III, "Education in Relation to the Christianisation of National Life", discusses the positioning of Protestant mission education in the mission fields towards a leadership training strategy and higher education institutions. Commission V, "The Preparation of Missionaries", proposes enhancing the academic standard of missionary training by incorporating language studies, the history of religions and the sociology of mission territories. It also discusses the need for centralized interdenominational mission training colleges and vernacular theological and Christian education.[1] Edinburgh 1910 also called for the development of contextualized forms of theological formation, which has been "in part answered in the twentieth century by the establishment and implementation of indigenous models of theological education and contextual theologies."[2]

The impulse of the vision on theological formation expressed at Edinburgh 1910 was channelled into the churches through the workings of the IMC and its national constituents such as the NCC. The latter formed the Committee on Theological Education (CTE) in 1924. The key focus of the CTE was training indigenous ministers of churches in the region.[3] In 1930, the IMC, in collaboration with the NCC, constituted the Commission on Christian Higher Education in India and Burma to review "the field of service open to the Christian colleges" in India and "to suggest ways in which the available resources of the Church can be more effectively used for this purpose."[4] The commission comprised representatives from the Conference of British Missionary Societies, the Foreign Mission Conference of North America and the NCC.[5] The commission's findings show a negative conclusion on the evangelistic efficacy of Christian colleges in India.[6] It suggests that to stay relevant, Christian colleges should "add to their present function of teaching the students within their walls the further function of supplying the community and the Christian church in particular with the knowledge they need for the solution of their problems."[7] Theological education was not mentioned in the original term in which the commission was constituted. However, at the request of the NCC, higher theological colleges and seminaries were included in the study.[8] The commission recommended the following suggestions as "the way of progress" for theological education in India:

> [i] Such co-operative effort as may help to set the teaching of the colleges free from narrow denominationalism and may make it possible to concentrate in the colleges a strong group of able Indian and non-Indian teachers; [ii] the encouragement in every way possible of the production of books in the vernaculars, suitable for the education of pastors and the maintenance of their cultural and Christian life; ... [iii]

---

[1] Dietrich Werner, "Theological Education in the Changing Context of World Christianity – an Unfinished Agenda" in *International Bulletin of Missionary Research* 35:2 (April 2011), 92.
[2] Werner, "Theological Education in the Changing Context of World Christianity, 96.
[3] C.W. Ranson, *The Christian Minister in India: His Vocation and His Training* (Madras: CLS, 1945), 1.
[4] *Report of the Commission on Christian Higher Education in India: An Enquiry into the Place of the Christian College in Modern India* (London: Oxford University Press, 1931), 2.
[5] The Commission consisted of A.D. Lindsay and Oscar M. Buck as Chairman and Secretary respectively, S.N. Mukerji and S.K. Datta as representatives of the NCC, Arthur W. Davies and Nicol Macnicol as representatives of British missionary societies, and William Adams Brown and William J. Hutchins as representatives of the North American missionary societies.
[6] *Report of the Commission on Christian Higher Education in India*, 96-120.
[7] *Ibid.* 232.
[8] *Ibid.* 234; Ranson, *The Christian Minister in India*, 1.

relate the teaching given to the actual life of the people and make it clear to those under instruction, by practical training, that Christianity is a way by which men and women in India may be helped to live their common lives and to serve each other.[9]

The commission's recommendations generated much discussion in India concerning cooperation in theological institutions, the strategic location of higher education institutions and the establishment of vernacular union schools of theology in key language areas.[10]

The discussion at the IMC Tambaram in 1938 provided further impetus to the conversation. During the conference, the younger churches expressed dissatisfaction with the existing system of training for Christian ministry. Many voiced the need "to arrange for the preparation of detailed studies of the situation, where these have not already been made, to visit the main centres of theological education and to work out a policy and programme for the training of the ministry in the younger churches."[11] However, the outbreak of the Second World War "rendered comprehensive international action" on the matter impossible. Nevertheless, in India, recognizing the urgency of the need to evaluate the theological education system, as expressed at Tambaram, the NCC initiated a survey on theological education. In its meeting at Nagpur from December 28, 1939, to January 2, 1940, the council instructed the CTE to investigate and report on the state of theological education in India to suggest areas of improvement, including "possibilities of cooperation in the work of training ministers all over India."[12] The commission worked amidst the disruptions of the World War and the cloud of an uncertain future that hung over India in the light of the national movement. It published its findings in 1945 under the title *The Christian Minister in India*, edited by C.W. Ranson, the then secretary of the NCC.[13]

The commission recognized the conundrum faced by the Indian Christian community of the time regarding whether the national government in independent India "will be entirely friendly or wholly antipathetic to the Church."[14] In a statement that turned out to be prophetic of the developments in independent India, the report of the commission stated,

> The apprehension felt by some Christians regarding the possibility of hostile or obstructive legislation by a future national government is not altogether unfounded. Already in certain Indian States such legislation has been enacted; and recent

---

[9] *Report of the Commission on Christian Higher Education in India*, 240-1. The report also adds, "and also of the production of books in English as well which shall aim at the translation of Christian ideas into the forms of Indian thought and the relation of the Indian religious heritage to the Christian heritage of the West" (240).
[10] Ranson, *The Christian Minister in India*, 2.
[11] "Findings of the International Missionary Council Meeting at Tambaram, Madras, December 1938"; Ranson, *The Christian Minister in India*, 3.
[12] Ranson, *The Christian Minister in India*, 3-4.
[13] *Ibid.*
[14] *Ibid.* 63. Ranson elaborates the challenge Indian Christians of the time faced as follows: "The association of Christianity with the ruling foreign power has aroused suspicion among certain sections of the Indian people, and has helped to foster the widespread idea that to become a Christian is in some sense a denial of Indian culture, a betrayal of *swadharma*, and, therefore, an act of disloyalty to the national cause." (64).

developments in certain public bodies in British India suggest that the majority community, in a self-governing India, may press for State action which will hamper the church in its evangelistic task. The Christian Church may thus find itself engaged in a struggle for the maintenance of religious freedom.[15]

The commission, however, urged not to "panic or dismay" but that the Indian Christian community "must prepare for it in a spirit of quiet confidence in God and with a recognition that the Christian faith requires those who are held by it something more than a timid defensive attitude towards the State and the great non-Christian communities."[16] The commission also suggested the importance of taking into account issues related to the urban-rural dynamics in Indian Christianity, secularism, social concerns and Christian apologetics in theological formation.[17]

In a damning assessment of the prevailing theological institutions, the commission reported that "[w]ith very few exceptions, they [were] ill-equipped to provide the Church with the well-trained ministry" that is required. It also reported that "denominational institutions frequently attempt training without the staff and the financial resources essential to efficiency, and without a steady supply of candidates of the right quality." Furthermore, it reported "much duplication of independent effort and a great deal of wasteful overlapping" in the way theological institutions functioned.[18] The commission invoked the discussion at Tambaram to recognize that "for many of the problems of theological education the corporate unity of the Church is the only solution." Tambaram had strongly asserted that the lack of cooperation between the theological institutions of denominational churches is a major hindrance: "One of the difficulties by which we are faced is the large number of small, isolated and ill-staffed institutions, in which the standard of work is inevitably low. It is our firm conviction that in almost every case theological training should be attempted except on a co-operative basis, with a number of churches participating."[19] The commission, therefore, put forward the following two suggestions: first, "theological training in theological schools and colleges should be planned as a joint enterprise of the whole Church, and should be carried out by the fullest possible cooperation of the churches in each area"; and second, "in order to facilitate such cooperation, where churches of widely differing traditions in doctrine, discipline and worship are working together, it may be necessary, through the system of halls or of federated colleges or in some other way, to provide adequately for the training of the students of those churches in the doctrines and traditions of their churches."[20] This suggestion for union institutions for theological education was not necessarily a novelty in India. Already in 1910, the United Theological College (UTC) was formed through cooperation between the United Free Church of Scotland, the American Arcot

---

[15] *Ibid.* 65.
[16] *Ibid.*
[17] *Ibid.* 66-74.
[18] *Ibid.* 145.
[19] "Findings of the International Missionary Council Meeting at Tambaram, Madras, December 1938."
[20] Ranson, *The Christian Minister in India*, 158.

Mission, the American Board of Commissioners for Foreign Missions, the Wesleyan Methodist Society and the London Missionary Society.[21] Nevertheless, union colleges such as UTC were an exception at the time rather than the norm, and therefore, the commission expressed the need to establish more such institutions.

The commission also worked closely with existing theological colleges towards partnership and cooperation. It envisioned "an all-Indian system of theological education, planned as a joint enterprise of the whole Church."[22] Towards this end, the NCC constituted the Board of Theological Education (BTE) in 1955, intending to bring together unaffiliated Bible schools and seminaries in India. At the time, the Senate of Serampore College was the only agency validating theological training in India. In the 1970s, the BTE and the Senate had a series of joint consultations resulting in the formation of the Board of Theological Education of the Senate of Serampore College (BTESSC) in 1975, which was to act as the "One National Structure for Theological Education in India."[23]

The 1950s saw an important development in the IMC, which had a lasting impact on theological formation in many parts of the world, including India. At the IMC Ghana in 1958, it established the Theological Education Fund (TEF) with the stated aim of training Christian ministers in the lands of the younger churches. Dietrich Werner points out three "major programmatic concerns" of the TEF:

> [i] for quality in theological education, ensured by a combination of intellectual rigor, spiritual maturity, and commitment; [ii] for authenticity, the result of a critical encounter with each cultural context in the design and purpose of theological education; and [iii] for creativity in theological education, which was understood as the promotion of new approaches through which the churches could act in obedience in mission.[24]

The TEF initiative found fertile ground in the changing context of newly independent countries such as India since the prevailing sense of national identity and awareness of contextual reality encourages contextual theological reflection. Therefore, as H.S. Wilson puts it, the TEF's promotion of contextualization of theological education was a "visionary mandate" that provided an "impetus to indigenization and inculturation efforts in Asia."[25] In India, the subsequent years saw the emergence of Dalit, Tribal, women's and other such theologies giving voice to local theologies.

---

[21] Vijay Kumar, "Ecumenical Cooperation of the Missions in Karnataka (India), 1834-1989: A Historical Analysis of the Evangelistic Strategy of the Missions" (PhD diss., Lutheran School of Theology, Chicago, 1996), 112.
[22] Ranson, *The Christian Minister in India*, 200-1.
[23] *Constitution – One national Structure for Theological Education in India.* (Serampore: Senate of Serampore College and the BTESSC, 2005).
[24] Werner, "Theological Education in the Changing Context of World Christianity," 93.
[25] H.S. Wilson, "Theological Education and Ecumenical Challenges in Asia," in *Asian Handbook for Theological Education and Ecumenism*, ed. Hope Antone et al (Oxford: Regnum, 2013), 628.

Seminaries, Cooperation and Collaboration

Theological education in India before the arrival of European missionaries appears to have followed a pattern similar to the *guru-chela*[26] ideal of Hindu tradition. The training of young boys ordained to the diaconate consists of living together as members of the family of an experienced priest for several years. During this stay, they acquire knowledge of the liturgy, the Bible and other practical matters of parish work from their mentor. At the end of the training, they were ordained as priests.[27]

The Franciscans founded the first theological seminary in India at Cranganore in 1540. In 1549, the Jesuit missionary Francis Xavier described it as "a really fine Seminary where as many as a hundred Indian students were formed in piety and learning."[28] Thus, from very early on, the Roman Catholic Church in India maintained theological seminaries, which continue even today. The Conference of Catholic Bishops of India (CCBI), the apex Roman Catholic organization in India, has its Commission for Vocations, Seminaries, Clergy and Religious (CVSCR) to coordinate the promotion and training of priests and religious. Further coordination and cooperation between Catholic seminaries are provided by the Association of Rectors of the Major Seminaries (ARMS), which facilitates the mutual sharing of resources between seminaries.[29] The Catholic seminaries, as elsewhere, remain in-house and run closely with their ecclesiastical hierarchy.

Seminary training akin to its contemporary usage was introduced in the Orthodox Church in India, first by the Roman Catholics and then by the Anglicans. The Roman Catholic mission started a seminary at Vaipicottah in 1584 (a college had existed since 1581), where both Latin and Syriac were taught to Syrian Christian students.[30] In 1815, with assistance from the British Resident Colonel John Munro and missionaries of the Church Mission Society (CMS), Mar Dionysius II started the Orthodox Theological Seminary (better known as the "Old Seminary"),[31] which set into motion the development of contemporary Orthodox seminaries in India. All branches of Orthodox churches in India – Malankara Orthodox Syrian Church, Malankara Mar Thoma Syrian Church and St. Thomas Evangelical Church of India – run seminaries. They also partner with other ecumenical and evangelical seminaries. The Mar Thoma Church, for instance, was one of the participants in establishing the Kerala United Theological Seminary (KUTS) in 1943 as a union institution.[32] The Jubilee

---

[26] *Chela* is a Sanskrit word for student or disciple of a religious *guru* or teacher.
[27] Ranson, *The Christian Minister in India*, 18.
[28] Quoted in Ranson, *The Christian Minister in India*, 21.
[29] "Vocations, Seminaries, Clergy and Religious", accessed February 4, 2023, https://ccbi.in/vocations-seminaries-clergy-and-religious/.
[30] Ranson, *The Christian Minister in India*, 21.
[31] Philip Kuruvilla, *Identity and Integration of the Orthodox Church in India* (Delhi: ISPCK, 2000), 60. The decision to open "a school of theology" was made by the church in 1809. The foundation stone was laid on February 18, 1813, and the construction completed in 1815. "Old Seminary (Pazhaya Seminary), Kottayam", accessed March 8, 2023, https://mosc.in/pilgrimcentres/old-seminary-pazhaya-seminary-kottayam.
[32] "Our Motto: Formation for Transformation", accessed February 4, 2023, https://kuts.edu.in/.

Memorial Bible College of the St. Thomas Evangelical Church is not only affiliated with the Asia Theological Association (ATA), an evangelical accrediting body, but also welcomes students from various church traditions.[33]

Most of the Protestant seminaries in India fall under BTESSC and ATA. The formation of the BTESSC as an ecumenical body has already been noted above. The ATA, formed in 1970, has emerged as the leading accrediting body among the evangelicals, with the patronage of the World Evangelical Fellowship (WEF), monitoring and regulating evangelical theological education in India.[34] Besides BTESSC and ATA, other accrediting agencies of theological education in India include the National Association of Theological Accreditation (NATA); the Senate of Indian Institute of Missiology (IIM), the Pentecostal Association for Theological Accreditation (PATA), the Baptist Association for Theological Accreditation (BATA) and the International Association for Theological Accreditation (IATA). Many theological colleges are not affiliated with any of these accrediting agencies, some of which even reject the accreditation concept.

Another aspect of theological education in India is its relations with secular universities. The history of this relation goes back to the nineteenth-century establishment of Serampore College as a university, the first in India, through the Royal Charter of King Frederick VI of Denmark in 1827 and confirmed by the British Government of India in 1845. The college itself was founded in 1818. From 1915 it began to offer degrees in divinity.[35] Currently, there are two ways in which theological education relates to universities in India: First, through a theological college obtaining affiliations to offer university degrees. For instance, the South Asia Institute of Advance Christian Studies (SAIACS) offers post-graduate degrees in Christian Studies as a study centre of Mysore University. Second, through degree programmes offered by universities under the University Grants Commission (UGC) such as the Martin Luther Christian University (MLCU), the Sam Higginbottom Institute of Agriculture, Technology and Science (SHIATS) and the North East Christian University (NECU), which offer degrees in Christian Studies. Department of Christianity in universities such as the Madras University and the Mysore University also provides avenues for the "scientific and comparative" study of Christianity at the post-graduate level.[36]

In 2020, the Government of India proposed a New Education Policy (NEP 2020), which envisions a centralised regulatory system of higher education in India where "the distinct functions of regulation, accreditation, funding, and

---

[33] "About JMBC", accessed February 4, 2023, http://jmbc.ac.in/about-jmbc-2/.
[34] "Asian Theological Association India", accessed February 1, 2023, https://ataindia.org/#:~:text=Overview%20of%20ATA,were%20begun%20for%20member%20institutions.
[35] Ravi Tiwari, "Senate of Serampore College (University) at ninety: Issues and Concerns", accessed February 1, 2023, https://www.senateofseramporecollege.edu.in/assets/uploads/cms_pdf/15939425421586079583Seramporeat_ninety.pdf.
[36] "Faculty of Arts: Christianity", accessed February 1, 2023, https://uni-mysore.ac.in/english-version/christianity; "Department of Christian Studies", accessed February 1, 2023, https://www.unom.ac.in/index.php?route=department/department/deptpage&deptid=19.

academic standard setting will be performed by distinct, independent, and empowered bodies."[37] It proposes the setting up of four "independent verticals within one umbrella institution," the Higher Education Commission of India (HECI): (i) National Higher Education Regulatory Council (NHERC), (ii) National Accreditation Council (NAC), (iii) Higher Education Grants Council (HEGC) and (iv) General Education Council (GEC).[38] The NEP 2020 speaks of educational reform in India, drawing from India's national heritage to become a "Global knowledge Superpower." However, it has caused uneasiness due to its lack of clarity on the future of minority community institutions such as theological seminaries and madrasas and the possible saffronization of education in India. Where do theological institutions fall within this new system? What will happen to theological degrees offered by institutions affiliated with Indian universities? These are questions, among others, for Indian theological institutions to address in the near future.

There is a plethora of institutions offering theological courses to the continuing demand for seminary education in India. They provide services to various levels of demands, from doctoral studies to vocational training, in English to vernacular, and on-campus to online courses. While some of these institutions have sufficient resources – material, personnel, recognition, network and others – to offer quality education, others do not. There are examples of mutual sharing of resources between theological colleges in India, one of which is the Joint Library Committee (JLC), a consortium of libraries of both Catholic and Protestant seminaries in Bangalore. Nevertheless, the relationships between theological seminaries or networks of seminaries in India are somewhat fragmented along various Christian traditions or tribal affiliations. Theological education in contemporary India is offered through denominational, non-denominational, evangelical and ecumenical seminaries. Institutions and accrediting agencies have no shared system towards common quality standards and mutual recognition. The dream of "One National Structure for Theological Education in India," therefore, remains unfulfilled. In light of the current composition of Christian traditions and theological institutions in India, what does "One National Structure" entail/include? The formation of the Asia Forum for Theological Education (AFTE) in 2011 can be a pointer for discussions in India.[39] In a communiqué issued during its first meeting on June 10-11, 2011, at the Trinity Theological College, Singapore, the participants affirmed: "that there is need for greater solidarity between different churches transcending stereotyped views of each other as 'ecumenical', 'evangelicals' or 'charismatic' in witnessing to Christ in today's world." Such solidarity, they affirmed, is

---

[37] *National Education Policy 2020* (Minister of Human Resource Development, Government of India), 47.
[38] *National Education Policy 2020*, 47.
[39] Participants of the first AFTE meeting came from the following associations and networks of theological education: SSC (SCEPTRE), ATESEA, PTCA, PERSETIA, APTA, ATA, KAATS, FTE, WCC-ETE, ATEM, MATS, PATS, BIT Thailand, Vietnamese Christian Mission (or VTC California).

Towards a *Metanoia* in Theological Formation

The regional consultation of the IMC/CWME Centenary Study Process takes note of the lived reality in India that makes minority communities like Christians uneasy. The challenge of the dominant Hindu right-wing idea of creating a homogenous India overshadowed the discussion in the consultation. Questions were also raised against the twentieth-century optimism on the belief that there is an inclusivist relativistic culture among the Hindu majority in India. Recent studies, however, show that the dominant fundamentalist Hindu right-wing groups follow a rigid exclusivist policy. They envision a homogeneous India, where homogeneity is identified with conformity to Hindu culture. Refusal to conform to their idea of homogeneity is considered anti-national and exclusivist; therefore, there is also a counteraccusation of minoritarian exclusivism. Thus, in India, both the majority and the minority stand accused of exclusivism. This is the tension within which Christian missions and relationships operate in India today. In light of this, the participants of the regional consultation expressed the need for a *metanoia*, a transformation, a critical evaluation of the way Christian people in India think of themselves.[41] This entails engagement and dialogue with people of other faiths, not just as an exercise of finding commonalities, but a critical evaluation of one's own faith, whereby the identity of the church is essentially a witness, an engagement and of dialogue, committed to driving itself and all other traditions back to the true faith. How does theological formation cater to such needs?

First, training the whole people of God. Wilson helpfully points out that the purpose of theological education "is to equip and instil self-realization of one's discipleship, and a lifelong commitment to transformation and liberation not only of oneself, but of all the peoples of God and the whole of creation from the perspective of the gospel of Jesus Christ." Theological training, therefore, should "equip the candidates both for ministry and mission within and beyond [the] Christian community."[42] In light of this goal, Wilson speaks of two equally important components in theological education:

> One is a cognitive part of providing knowledge about Christianity with input on Bible, theology, history of Christianity and Pastoral practices, integrated as much as possible. The other ... is to equip the ministerial candidates with practical skills to engage with the community, both for the sake of nurturing Christian community/congregation (that one is responsible) and to minister towards building

---

[40] "Asian Forum on Theological Education (AFTE): Communiqué", accessed February 4, 2023, https://www.oikoumene.org/resources/documents/asian-forum-on-theological-education-afte.
[41] "Report of the ATC-UTC-SAIACS-Conference in the IMC Centenary Study Process 2021-22."
[42] Wilson, "Theological Education and Ecumenical Challenges in Asia," 625-6.

a holistic relationship with community at large for the enrichment of all the members of a given society.[43]

Theological formation should equip people not just with the history and text of our faith but also impart knowledge of social problems and the means to engage with them. Furthermore, the scope of theological formation goes beyond the training of the seminarians and into the nurturing and equipping of the whole people of God. This idea was affirmed in the Manila Consultation on Ecumenical Theological Education on August 10-14, 2004. A. Wati Longchar summarises the vision expressed in the consultation as follows:

> Therefore, the vision of ecumenical education cannot be narrowly confined to ministerial training programs of churches alone; rather it involves equipping the whole people of God. It is Laos – the whole people of God. It is an ongoing process in which the whole people of God are empowered for formation and transformation of all communities. It searches to build a just and inclusive community in the context of the people of other faiths and ideologies.[44]

In a similar vein, writing in the *Journal of Asian Evangelical Theology*, Bruce Nicholls insists that the objective of theological education should be equipping the whole people of God and that training the laity is vital to the mission of the Indian church.[45] Thus, there is an already existing continuum of advocacy among theological educators in India for the theological formation of the whole people of God, that theological formation should cease being pastor or leader-oriented and become congregation and community-oriented. There are also courses available that provide theological education for lay Christians, such as TAFTEE's lay training programmes[46] and SAIACS's Bible for All (BFA), which make it possible for lay people to pursue theological education. How may lay theological formation be further encouraged? Are the existing curriculums set to meet the needs of lay ministry as an authentic Christian witness? A closer examination of the current curriculum will be required for a better assessment. However, to cite an example, Atul Aghamkar speaks of how the current curriculum does not prepare one to engage in informal dialogue. Informal dialogue is "part and parcel" of daily experience in India, yet, Aghamkar posits, "very little attention is given to informing, equipping, and mobilizing Christians in India to undertake such informal dialogue with people of other faiths."[47] An all-India commission or consultation, similar to the one initiated by the IMC and the NCC in the 1930s and 40s, will be a welcome move to examine how theological formation in India might pragmatically address the call to engage in training the whole people of God.

---

[43] Wilson, "Theological Education and Ecumenical Challenges in Asia," 631.
[44] A. Wati Longchar, ed. *Ecumenical Theological Education in Changing Context: Problems, Challenges and Hope* (Rajabari: ETC-WCC/CAA, 2004), 9-10.
[45] Bruce Nicholls, "New Horizons for Theological Education in Today's changing World," in *Journal of Asian Evangelical Theology* 11 (June-Dec. 2003), 63.
[46] Vinay Samuel and Chris Sugden, "TAFTEE: An Indian Approach to Training for Ministry," in *International Review of Mission* 71:282 (April 1982), 172-8.
[47] Atul Aghamkar, "Hindu-Christian Dialogue in India," in EAST MEETS EAST: In the Heartland of Hinduism Evangelical Interfaith Dialogue 2:2 (2011), https://fullerstudio.fuller.edu/featured-article-hindu-christian-dialogue-in-india/.

Second, working together with the church. Speaking at the convocation service of the Senate of Serampore at the Tamilnadu Theological Seminary, Madurai, on February 2, 1980, Chandran Devanesan suggests that theological colleges ought to play a "prophetic ministry to the church": "There is ... the need for a simultaneous prophetic ministry that seeks to reform the Church along with the prophetic ministry of the Church to the World."[48] There is a dual prophetic ministry in which both churches and theological institutions play the role of prophets and work together to read the signs of the day and act accordingly. However, churches and theological institutions in India do not always seem to sing from the same hymn sheet. There is a disconnect between the churches and theological institutions, whereby while the former has been accused of refusing to accept any change to tradition, the latter has been accused of being oblivious to the daily spiritual and lived realities of the Christian masses.[49] Joshva Raja argues for the need for a "Theology of Creative and Fruitful Tension," whereby the "theological community may recognise the churches' theologies which are often concerned with people's faith and traditions (theology from above) whereas the churches may realise the importance of challenging some of the traditional ways of understanding faith and life to relate it to their context (theology from below)."[50] Churches and theological institutions, as J.G. Muthuraj points out, are "friends, partners and critics."[51] The prophetic mission of theological education involves, on the one hand, identifying blind spots in the vision of the church and suggesting correctives and innovations, and on the other hand, listening to the heartbeat of the church and helping the church equip itself to do its mission.

The participants of the regional consultation were conscious of paying attention to the pulse of the Indian churches. Certain observations were made of the nature and yearnings of the Indian churches during the consultation, which can be pointers for the future direction of theological formation in India:

(i) The participants recognized that in many churches in India, the passion for evangelism is engrained in the lifeblood of the church.[52] Raja brings out the raw reality of the difference in focus between the churches and theological institutions in India when he states that while the major concern of the churches is to "evangelise the masses ... theological colleges are concerned with dialogue between different religions."[53] Theological educators cannot afford to overlook the deep conviction towards evangelism among the people in the pew. How do we balance equipping Christian people to follow their conviction for evangelism

---

[48] Chandran D. S. Devanesan, "Theological Education: Retrospect and Prospect", accessed February 1, 2023, https://biblicalstudies.org.uk/pdf/ijt/30-1_001.pdf.
[49] Joshva Raja, "Relevant and Effective Theological Education in the Twenty First Century India," in *The Asbury Theological Journal* 60:1 (Spring 2005), 116.
[50] *Ibid.* 116.
[51] Quoted in Raja, "Relevant and Effective Theological Education in the Twenty First Century India," 115.
[52] Report of the ATC-UTC-SAIACS-Conference in the IMC Centenary Study Process 2021-22.
[53] Raja, "Relevant and Effective Theological Education in the Twenty First Century India," 115.

while cautioning them on the intricacies involved in doing missions in a multireligious context? Here, a helpful reference point is the WCC's "Guidelines on dialogue with the people of other faiths and ideologies," which, while recognizing that Christians should "witness fully to their deepest conviction," asserts that it should be done within the framework of a long-term approach of living together with people of various traditions and faiths.[54] This leads us to the second observation, which is,

(ii) There is a desire among Christian people in India to live in harmony with their neighbours of other faiths. In this regard, two ideas were expressed strongly in the regional consultation: (a) a shift towards informal dialogue (while also acknowledging the importance of formal dialogue) and (b) the need to live an authentic Christian life as a witness to the truth.[55] If this is the direction for the churches and Christian missions in India, what should theological formation look like? How might theological institutions simulate the reality of interfaith engagement as a daily experience in India?

(iii) The task of equipping Christian people to engage in nation-building: the participants of the regional consultation took encouragement from the past, whereby Christian missions have contributed to nation-building in areas such as education, social reforms, economic development and others.[56] Going forward, how might theological education equip people with tools to tackle social, political and economic problems today? Should theological curriculum include subjects such as law, medicine, management and so on?

Theological educators and institutions need to play a prophetic role in preparing churches to engage meaningfully with contemporary issues. The WCC global study report on theological education (2009) underlines the conviction that,

> theological education is the seedbed for the renewal of churches, their ministries and mission and their commitment to church unity in today's world. If theological education systems are neglected or not given their due prominence in church leadership, in theological reflection and in funding, consequences might not be visible immediately, but quite certainly will become manifest after one or two decades in terms of theological competence of church leadership, holistic nature of the churches mission, capacities for ecumenical and interfaith dialogue and for dialogue between churches and society.[57]

This statement aligns with the long-standing tradition of the IMC process that has highlighted the strategic importance of theological education in any mission

---

[54]"Guidelines on dialogue with the people of other faiths and ideologies", accessed February 1, 2023, https://www.oikoumene.org/resources/documents/guidelines-on-dialogue-with-people-of-living-faiths-and-ideologies.

[55] Report of the ATC-UTC-SAIACS-Conference in the IMC Centenary Study Process 2021-22.

[56] Report of the ATC-UTC-SAIACS-Conference in the IMC Centenary Study Process 2021-22.

[57]"Theological education, seedbed for churches' renewal", accessed February 1, 2023, https://www.oikoumene.org/news/theological-education-seedbed-for-churches-renewal; Todd M. Johnson and Kenneth Ross, eds. *Atlas of Global Christianity, 1910-2010* (Edinburgh: Edinburgh University Press, 2009), 107.

strategy. The engagement of the IMC process in India over the years has also shown the importance of periodic evaluation of the standard and content of theological education to ensure that it plays a prophetic role. When times and issues change, the case for theological formation also needs to be reconsidered, if not reconstructed. The current situation in India indicates that Christian people will be increasingly called upon to prove the authenticity of their faith and justify the motive of their missions. Therefore, the theological formation will have to look beyond ministerial formation and invest in the lives of the people of God to be authentic witnesses. This will require cooperation and united effort between churches and seminaries and between theological educators and institutions of all Christian traditions.

Contributors

Ajay Chakraborty is Associate Professor of History of Christianity and the Principal of Satchitanand Dharmashastra Vidyapeeth, Raipur, Chhattisgarh, India.

Arvind Kumar is a Research Scholar in the Department of History of Christianity, the United Theological College (UTC), Bangalore, India.

John Arun Kumar is Professor of Religious Studies. He has served as faculty and the Head of the Department of Intercultural and Religious Studies at the South Asia Institute of Advance Christian Studies (SAIACS), Bangalore, India.

Zadingluaia Chinzah hails from Lawngtlai in Southern Mizoram and is an ordained minister of the Lairam Jesus Christ Baptist Church. He is a doctoral researcher in the Department of History of Christianity, SATHRI, Senate of Serampore College.

Chongpongmeren Jamir is a Postdoctoral Fellow in Church History at the Inez and Julius Polin Institute, Åbo Akademi University, Turku, Finland. He has served as faculty at the South Asia Institute of Advanced Christian Studies (SAIACS), Bangalore, India.

H. Lalrinthanga is Professor of History of Christianity and the Dean of Postgraduate Studies at the Aizawl Theological College (ATC), Aizawl, India.

Taimaya Ragui is a tribal-indigenous theologian from Ukhrul, India. He works with The Shepherd's Academy of Oxford Centre for Religion and Public Life, Oxford, UK.

Lalfakawma Ralte is a faculty in the Department of History of Christianity at the United Theological College (UTC), Bangalore, India.

E.D. Solomon is Professor and Head of the Department of Missiology at the Caleb Institute, Farrukhnager, Gurgaon-NCR Delhi, India. He is an ordained minister of the Mennonite Brethren Church of India. He has taught at both the Senate of Serampore College and Asia Theological Association affiliated schools such as the Mennonite Brethren Bible College, Telangana and the South Asia Institute of Advance Christian Studies (SAIACS), Bangalore.

Francis Thonippara, CMI, is Professor and the Head of the Department of Church History at Dharmaram Vidya Kshetram (DVK), Bangalore, India. In 2019 Pope Francis nominated him as a member of the Pontifical Committee for Historical Sciences, Holy See, Vatican, for a period of five years. He was the President of DVK and Provincial Superior of CMI St. Thomas Province, Kozhikode.

Kaholi Zhimomi is Associate Professor in the Department of History of Christianity, the United Theological College (UTC), Bangalore, India.